Now, Voyager

Wisconsin/Warner Bros. Screenplay Series

Now, Voyager

Edited with an introduction by

Jeanne Thomas Allen

Published for the Wisconsin Center for Film and Theater Research by
The University of Wisconsin Press

Published 1984

The University of Wisconsin Press
114 North Murray Street
Madison, Wisconsin 53715

The University of Wisconsin Press, Ltd.
1 Gower Street
London WC1E 6HA England

First printing

Printed in the United States of America

For LC CIP information see the colophon

ISBN 0-299-09790-0 cloth; ISBN 0-299-09794-3 paper

Contents

Foreword

In donating the Warner Film Library to the Wisconsin Center for Film and Theater Research in 1969, along with the RKO and Monogram film libraries and UA corporate records, United Artists created a truly great resource for the study of American film. Acquired by United Artists in 1957, during a period when the major studios sold off their films for use on television, the Warner library is by far the richest portion of the gift, containing eight hundred sound features, fifteen hundred short subjects, nineteen thousand still negatives, legal files, and press books, in addition to screenplays for the bulk of the Warner Brothers product from 1930 to 1950. For the purposes of this project, the company has granted the Center whatever publication rights it holds to the Warner films. In so doing, UA has provided the Center another opportunity to advance the cause of film scholarship.

Our goal in publishing these Warner Brothers screenplays is to explicate the art of screenwriting during the thirties and forties, the so-called Golden Age of Hollywood. In preparing a critical introduction and annotating the screenplay, the editor of each volume is asked to cover such topics as the development of the screenplay from its source to the final shooting script, differences between the final shooting script and the release print, production information, exploitation and critical reception of the film, its historical importance, its directorial style, and its position within the genre. He is also encouraged to go beyond these guidelines to incorporate supplemental information concerning the studio system of motion picture production.

We could set such an ambitious goal because of the richness of the script files in the Warner Film Library. For many film titles, the files might contain the property (novel, play, short story, or original story idea), research materials, variant drafts of scripts (from story outline to treatment to shooting script), post-production items such as press books and dialogue continuities, and legal records (details of the acquisition of the property, copyright registration, and contracts with actors and directors). Editors of the Wisconsin/Warner Bros. Screenplay Series receive copies of all the materials, along with prints of the films (the most authoritative ones available for reference purposes), to use in preparing the introductions and annotating the final shooting scripts.

In the process of preparing the screenplays for publication, typographical errors were corrected, punctuation and capitalization were modernized, and the format was redesigned to facilitate readability.

Unless otherwise specified, the photographs are frame enlargements taken from a 35-mm print of the film provided by United Artists.

In 1977 Warner Brothers donated the company's production records and distribution records to the University of Southern California and Princeton University, respectively. These materials are now available to researchers and complement the contents of the Warner Film Library donated to the Center by United Artists.

Tino Balio
General Editor

Introduction

Now, Voyager *as Women's Film: Coming of Age Hollywood Style*

Jeanne Thomas Allen

Bette Davis's performance as Charlotte Vale, daughter of a domineering Boston matriarch, in *Now, Voyager* (1942) offers something rare and vital in American mass culture: the story of a woman's struggle to gain initiation into adulthood and a relative measure of independence. Although social commentators have discussed the decline of significant initiation rites for American youth, there is little doubt that "coming of age in America" fiction flourishes from *Look Homeward, Angel* and "The Bear" to *The Catcher in the Rye* and *Lord of the Flies* or, more recently, *Ordinary People.* Yet finding a comparable body of literature or popular entertainment about the experiences of women seeking to be self-determining adults is a far more difficult task.[1]

1. Kay Mussell (*Women's Gothic and Romantic Fiction: A Reference Guide* [Westport, Connecticut: Greenwood Press, 1981], especially the introductions to chapters 1 and 5) argues that the primary "coming of age" fiction experience for women is contained in the romance genre. Apart from adolescent fiction (i.e., Nancy Drew and other modestly professional or amateur adventure novels), the only allowable means for female initiation into adulthood or separation from parents in American mass-culture fiction is through heterosexual romance. See also Beatrice Hofstadter, "Popular Culture and the Romantic Heroine," *American Scholar*, 30 (Winter, 1960/61):98–116.

Introduction

Although Olive Higgins Prouty's 1941 novel of the same title makes such a contribution, it is encased in a melodrama over-shadowed by a theme of romantic but frustrated love, which caused most critics of both novel and film to dismiss it as inconsequential. Indeed, critics have rarely perceived the importance of such women's initiation-ritual fiction, much less recognized it when it was offered. Whether or not it is the reason for the popular success and endurance of *Now, Voyager* as a film classic, this vivid presentation of a maturing, increasingly self-reliant woman bears up under the scrutiny of continued decades, claiming both our attention and need to explain its achievement.

How did this representation of a woman struggling to maturity emerge from the Hollywood film industry of the early 1940s? Several factors must be explored from the novel, which provided the initial material to the contributions of the collective institution of the American film industry as well as the structural and stylistic elements of films in this era of American studio production. Only recently has there been an attempt, made largely by feminist film critics, to salvage a number of Hollywood films of the thirties and forties which had been consigned to minor status under the heading of "women's films" or "the weepies."[2] Unlike the adventure films of swashbuckling heroes or hard-boiled detectives, "women's films" have been regarded derogatorily as escapist fare, providing an emotional catharsis by blending familiar experience and fantasy fulfillment.[3] Their explicit appeal to and ability to arouse emotional response were a sure sign of their trivial position. Critics like Higham and

2. Barbara Creed, "The Position of Women in Hollywood Melodramas," *Australian Journal of Screen Theory*, 4:27–31; Molly Haskell, *From Reverence to Rape* (Baltimore: Penguin, 1973); Mary Beth Haralovich, "Romance in the Hollywood Film and in Poster Publicity: Studio Years," unpublished doctoral dissertation, University of Wisconsin-Madison, 1984; Diane Waldman, "Horror and Domesticity: The Modern Gothic Romance Film of the 1940's," unpublished doctoral dissertation, University of Wisconsin-Madison, 1981.

3. Lawrence J. Quirk, *The Great Romantic Films* (Secaucus, New Jersey: Citadel Press, 1974).

Greenberg ("a triumph of Forties kitsch")[4] or Ted Sennett ("most blatantly sentimental, most 'woman's novellette-ish'")[5] or Pauline Kael ("great trash") express the disdain and grudging attraction in commentary about women's films and *Now, Voyager* in particular.

In their comments can be found the tension, if not embarrassment, of the critic confronted with the disturbingly forceful appeal of popular culture. The "women's films" focused on women's emotional lives, which critics often dispensed with as trivially sentimental. Few critics sifted the coincidental and manipulative plot constructions from the exploration of emotional conflicts and tensions at the center of many women's lives. Richard Corliss outlined the territory of *Now, Voyager* and indeed many "women's films": "Nearly every major character in "Now, Voyager" is either a parent figure, a spouse figure, or a child figure—or a combination of all three. Davis's Charlotte Vale, for instance, is at thirty-odd still her mother's unwanted baby, as well as her lover's mistress and the lover's daughter's surrogate mother. Claude Rains, the psychiatrist is both father to Davis and, if not a lover, certainly a very affectionate friend, just as Paul Heinreid, the married lover, acts as both psychiatrist and father figure. Even the love Davis and Heinreid share is a schizophrenic business."[6] Corliss's list of roles significantly omits woman as nurturing mother and as peer, which are at the *center* of the film's resolution. But his recognition that women's social roles are complex and frequently conflicting is important in understanding why such films are both significant and ignored. Most critics and commentators and perhaps the public see the everyday reality of women's social roles as schizophrenic without pausing to consider the sociological and ideological tensions behind these psychological conflicts.

4. Charles Higham and Joel Greenberg, *Hollywood in the Forties* (New York: A. S. Barnes, 1968), p. 144.

5. Ted Sennett, *Warner Brothers Presents* (New Rochelle, New York: Arlington House, 1971), pp. 135–36.

6. Richard Corliss, *Talking Pictures* (Woodstock, New York: Overlook Press, 1974), p. 289.

Introduction

The derogation from and discomfort of critics responding to films like *Now, Voyager* are not without exception, as we shall see in examining the documented reaction to the film. But they have a long history, a history which has generally failed to sort out the rather complicated dual quality of mass culture generated by or directed toward women: a source of confirmation and realization of the social and emotional realities of women's daily lives and a compensation, through consolation and fantasy, for the gaps, the absent options or alternatives in that range of experience.

Women's Fiction

Women writers and readers of popular fiction have been both derided for their sentimentality and, more recently, studied for their significance as a force in the rise of American mass culture of the nineteenth and twentieth centuries. At least since Nathaniel Hawthorne's reference to "those damned scribbling women" with Mrs. E.D.E.N. Southworth as lightning rod for his wrath, critics have bemoaned the saccharine prose of popular women writers. Serious women writers have fought lengthy battles to distinguish themselves from their "popular" counterparts. Indeed, Olive Higgins Prouty, who wrote *Now, Voyager,* confessed that the derogatory *Times Books Review* response of a woman reviewer putting her work in the class of "lady novelists" was "ruthless" enough to penetrate the tough hide she had cultivated to withstand adverse criticism as a writer.[7]

Regardless of the opinion of literary critics, the importance of the female middle-class audience to the rise of the novel is notable. Because women of the upper and middle classes were barred from the business affairs of men and from many of their leisure activities as well, such women had a great deal of leisure often occupied in "omnivorous reading."[8] Ann Douglas's recent study of the female audience for mass culture points out that

7. Olive Higgins Prouty, *Pencil Shavings* (Cambridge, Massachusetts: Riverside Press, 1961), p. 195.

8. Ann Douglas, *The Feminization of American Culture* (New York: Avon Books, 1977), p. 9.

12

women, disenfranchised from so many areas of production and performance by the late nineteenth century, were thoroughly ensconced in literary production and that the results of their labors were avidly consumed by generations of middle-class women. "Literature was functioning more and more as a form of leisure, a complicated dream-life in the busiest, most wide-awake society in the world." Among the many functions such reading performed, Douglas includes that of a "narcissistic self-education for those excluded from the harsh school of practical competition."[9]

Now, Voyager, as both novel and film, makes several references to women's fiction as a source of information for women whose worldliness and sophistication are restricted, if not precluded, by a patriarchal society. Prouty characterizes the illicit private life of twenty-eight-year-old "spinster" Charlotte Vale as filled with reading anything she could of Laurence, Proust, Hemingway, Maugham, Huxley, as well as Havelock Ellis and Bertrand Russell. But this appetite and taste were concealed, using volumes of Jane Austen, Emerson, and Thoreau to hide the *Decameron, Sons and Lovers,* and *Madame Bovary.*

Yet repeated references by Charlotte about her knowledge of how to behave socially, particularly with men, do not seem to be to this reading but to novels about women who lost "their inhibitions with liquor in isolated places with men." Charlotte's domineering Victorian mother finds such literature scandalous, Charlotte's upper-class Bostonian fiancé is disturbed at her interest, while Charlotte maintains, "It's life, it's about human beings," and her lover confirms this conviction by acting it out with her.

The predominantly dismissive attitude toward "women's fiction" helps to account for the similar dismissal of Olive Higgins Prouty's contribution to a film about an emergent, adult woman. Credit for such a characterization most frequently goes to Bette Davis, who certainly deserves considerable acclaim, and a host of other Hollywood transformations, completely overlooking the fact that many of the key scenes demonstrating the strength and

9. Ibid., p. 13.

independence of the maturing Charlotte Vale are directly lifted from Prouty's novel.

Olive Higgins Prouty

Olive Higgins was born and raised in Worcester, Massachusetts, the daughter of a college professor. Pursuing a commitment to writing by the time she graduated from Smith College, she determined to delay marriage and children until she had acquired both broader knowledge and experience and some measure of publication success. Courted by the eldest son of the owner of the "world's largest shoe factory," Olive put off his proposals until he agreed to move to Boston where she could enroll in creative writing courses at Radcliffe. These proved a spur to her ambition, and she achieved her goal of publication the same year she married, 1907, when she was twenty-six.

Dropping her ambition to work in New York City because of her mother's anemic condition, Olive Prouty published a series of stories based on her own family experience. "Nothing requiring great knowledge," she said. "Just little domestic things that I know all about."[10] By 1913 a collection of those "domestic things," centering about a character modeled on her sister, were published as a novel. Within weeks of the first edition, publicized to her husband's horror by electric lights on a busy Boston avenue, *Bobbie General Manager* went into second edition and her career seemed soundly launched.

Olive Prouty's attitude toward her writing as revealed in her memoirs seems ambivalent if not contradictory. Although she claimed in 1942 that writing was her hobby while her home was her career,[11] her delay of marriage for some five years while she worked as a writer and her description of her writing career argue something else. That she was wife, mother, daughter, and professional writer is significant given the impossibility of family roles being combined with career on the Hollywood screen, which adapted her work. Her willingness to space out her lit-

10. Prouty, *Pencil Shavings*, p. 123.
11. Ibid., pp. 136–53.

14

erary work over half a century with wide gaps between novels and her marriage to an extremely wealthy family help to account for this achievement.

But despite the apparent compatibility of writing and home-life, both continued at considerable personal cost. Her memoirs refer to her sense of guilt for pursuing her career—"so utterly selfish an expenditure of time for which I was receiving so much payment *unnecessary to our welfare*" (italics mine). Consequently, her husband (who arranged the terms of every writing contract, kept acounts of the proceeds, hired a lawyer, and handled business correspondence) suggested expiating her guilt by donating some of her proceeds to charity.[12] Prouty made the familiar concessions of professional women to husbands' egos such as discouraging publicity of her success and avoiding social situations that celebrated her fame outside the intimacy of the family.

Olive Prouty experienced a nervous breakdown two years after the death of her fourth and last child who was a year and a half old and the second of her children to die. Her breakdown was regarded as a weakness of character by her husband as by so many others. She stayed for a time at the Riggs Foundation at Stockbridge, where Dr. Riggs presented her with schedules and advice not unlike those provided Charlotte Vale by Dr. Jaquith. Perhaps most important, he also secured permission from her husband to have a place to write outside of her home. Her "office" gave a professional status to her work that money, public applause, and critical acclaim had not been sufficient to establish. Much of Prouty's experience of the guilts of the professional woman writer entered her characterization of Charlotte Vale. In the Vale trilogy she wrote about a New England family and again the "domestic things that [she knew] all about."

Now, Voyager, the Novel

Now, Voyager as described by Olive Higgins Prouty is the story of a "spinster who finally finds escape from the domination of her mother through doors opened by a nervous breakdown."

12. Ibid., p. 158.

The novel opens on shipboard just as Charlotte Vale has had her first encounter with her future lover, Jerry Durrance. Her skeptical and sarcastic attempts to dissuade his attentions are unsuccessful. His involvement with her deepens, based on their common interest in travel and similar family predicaments, which have resulted in nervous breakdowns for both. This is an important element of their kinship—not repeated in any subsequent script treatment—because they are peers emotionally, although Jerry's marital status provides a social confidence that Charlotte's ill-concealed spinsterhood does not.

The novel suggests through flashbacks that Charlotte's developing affair with Jerry repeats a previous shipboard romance when she was eighteen, which underlines Jerry's importance in restoring Charlotte's sense of being a desirable woman. This basis of her self-worth had been destroyed by her mother, who had pressured the other young man to withdraw and had then replaced him with herself as the object of Charlotte's devoted attention. Now at thirty, her low self-esteem is "cured" by the attentions of a man accompanied by social acceptance from other couples.

So armed, Charlotte returns from Europe to Boston to face her mother, a formidable matriarch who counts on Charlotte's lack of self-confidence and financial dependence to maintain her dominance. With her armor of advice from her psychiatrist, Dr. Jaquith, the moral support of friends, and the habits of sophistication European travel has provided, Charlotte takes on her mother and, as she says to Lisa at a family gathering, "wins the first round." Jerry returns from his "business vacation" and love affair to family responsibility. But with no advice from Dr. Jaquith, the truly authoritative "father" of the story, he is not able to confront the domineering "mother" of his life—his wife, Isobel. His inability to deal with that relationship is presented by Prouty as a noble and honorable loyalty. Though his love affair gives him some strength for professional self-realization, he does not challenge his personal and social domination as does Charlotte, whose social assertiveness leads her to sense a need for professional or financial independence: "I'm not afraid. Mother, I'm not afraid."

Charlotte turns her new-found energies to parenting Jerry's child, applying the knowledge Jaquith offered her to become the mother she needed as a child. And since it is one of Jaquith's patients she is caring for, she implicitly becomes a partner to Jaquith. Although the novel ends with Charlotte's insistence that caring for Tina unites her with Jerry through a sublimation of their love affair, character development suggests that Charlotte has outgrown the father-lover she met on the boat and become the peer of the father-doctor, joining in his work and supporting it.

Prouty's stories and novels had enjoyed considerable commercial and critical success before the appearance of *Now, Voyager* in 1941. Her short stories were published in *American Magazine, McClure's,* and *Everybody's* and were then collected in her first novel. Four other novels and collections of stories appeared between 1916 and 1919 before *Stella Dallas* (1922), her greatest popular and critical success. Well received by reviewers for the *London Times, Boston Transcript,* and *Times Review, Stella Dallas* enjoyed a particularly long life in numerous media forms: a Broadway play starring Mrs. Leslie Carter, a silent film starring Belle Bennett, later a Goldwyn talkie with Barbara Stanwyck, and finally a weekly radio serial that ran for fifteen years from 1938 until 1953.

These resurrections of *Stella Dallas* and its success were accompanied by the magazine serialization and book publication of the Vale trilogy, of which *Now, Voyager* is the third and last. The book was published October 8, 1941 by Houghton, Mifflin and Company. The Warner Brothers contract, issued to Prouty one week after her literary agent received the advance copy and before the luke-warm reviews and bookstore sales were evident, offered two installments of $20,000 each not only for *Now, Voyager* but for any material in *Lisa Vale* concerning the character, Charlotte Vale.[13] *Now, Voyager* did not do well commercially de-

---

13. Contract between Olive Higgins Prouty and Warner Bros. Pictures, Inc. (November 28, 1941) in the United Artists Collection, Record Group 1 of the Archives Division of the State Historical Society of Wisconsin, Madison, Wisconsin.

spite its sale to the Literary Guild and the Dell edition, which offered the paperback at 25¢ a copy. Prouty never collected the additional $10,000 which Warners offered if the book sold fifty thousand copies before May 1, 1942. The 763,327 copies total sold of *Now, Voyager* was half the number sold of her preceding novel *Lisa Vale*, despite the film's promotional effect. Unquestionably the speed with which Warners optioned and adapted her novel had much to do with the longevity and success of both *Stella Dallas* and *Lisa Vale*, which they hoped to exploit with *Now, Voyager*.

Warner Brothers' swiftness in optioning movie rights was matched in their speed of production. The finalized contract with Prouty dated November 28, 1941 after an October publication was followed by an end-of-the-year Treatment by Edmund Goulding, director of Bette Davis's earlier *Dark Victory*, while legal complications over the rights to *Lisa Vale* held off immediate production. A Revised Final script was completed by April 1942.

The history of these script versions of *Now, Voyager* is one of significant transformations that document the collective quality of the Hollywood industry's mode of production during the studio years. If not as Cinderella-like as Charlotte Vale's transformation from a "victim of domestic circumstances . . . to a self-reliant and successful woman," the script's changes afford documentation of the process of converting Prouty's instance of so-called "women's fiction" to the Hollywood "women's film" of the 1940s.

Edmund Goulding's Treatment

Edmund Goulding's Treatment was the first step in adapting Prouty's novel for Hollywood film-making. Since Goulding had directed Bette Davis in her two important films of 1939, *The Old Maid* and the public's favorite, *Dark Victory*, we might safely assume that his assignment to the Treatment followed Davis's insistence that she, not Irene Dunne, be cast in the lead. Since the studio agreed that Davis as a New England Yankee was aptly qualified to dramatize Charlotte, the studio's choice of Goulding made eminently good sense.

Goulding, who had been a writer himself and had gained the

reputation of being a "woman's director," suggested tightening the narrative line and making Charlotte and Jerry bolder and more resilient characters. He believed that the thread to develop was the basic premise of melodrama: "the grim opposition to the heroine's and the audience's deep desires."[14] The film, he argued, should begin with Mrs. Vale's disruption of Charlotte's adolescent romance with Leslie Trotter. Commenting on his sense of the novel's heroine, Goulding insisted that Charlotte be presented as "smouldering rather than passive, possessed of a deep resentment rather than passive acceptance,"[15] heightening the dramatic tension of opposition to such a woman's desires. Goulding perceived the scene in which Charlotte confronts her mother as "splendid," a remark he makes about no other scene in the novel, a compliment further paid by Casey Robinson in lifting it almost intact from the novel.

Goulding believed Jerry's previous breakdown was too much of a "coincidence," an assertion undercut by his recognition that millions of people know such duress. Goulding's refusal to make the lovers fellow sufferers suggests a general taboo in Hollywood films: male romantic leads do not have nervous breakdowns. Goulding's concern for male-lead characterization extends to his explanation for Jerry's inability to confront his domineering "parent"—his wife, Isobel. Goulding insists that Jerry is held by a will "not stronger than his own but so much weaker that it demands his complete loyalty."[16] He suggests not presenting Jerry's wife and daughters directly in the film, since "in light of modern day thinking, [they] would find an impatient intolerance on the part of the audience as to why the man insists upon this twist in the story."[17] Clearly the parallel between Charlotte and Jerry is discomforting to Goulding, who wants to make Jerry's warmth and understanding the compel-

---

14. Edmund Goulding, *Now, Voyager* Treatment, United Artists Collection, Record Group 1, Archives Division of the State Historical Society of Wisconsin, Madison, Wisconsin, 15 pp., unpaginated.

15. Ibid.

16. Ibid.

17. Ibid.

ling force behind Charlotte's reaching out to him, another father figure. Goulding begins the process of "strengthening" the male figures as father-doctors in Charlotte's rebirth, while the roles of Charlotte's sister-in-law, Lisa, and friend, Deb, are minimized. The psychological midwives of the novel are replaced by doctors, who turn the midwives into nurses, while Charlotte's woman enemies remain as vengeful in the scripts and film as in the novel.

Goulding's Treatment of the novel twice refers to Prouty's previous success with *Stella Dallas*, making it clear that Warners hoped to repeat its popularity by adapting Prouty's 1941 novel for the screen. Goulding sees in the relationship of Charlotte to Jerry's daughter Tina the "sacrificing mother" sentiment of *Stella Dallas*: "All the wallop of the author's craft at tears (remembering *Stella Dallas*)" and later when Charlotte's success at mothering is made evident to Jerry—"it is then that the picture should have all the qualities and more emotionally of 'Stella Dallas,' the effect of which upon an audience has seldom been equalled."[18]

Casey Robinson's Screenplay

Casey Robinson, paired with Goulding and Davis in several previous films, was the Warners' screenwriter assigned to *Now, Voyager*. Having started work in 1928 for Paramount, Robinson was brought to Warners by Harry Joe Brown, who had directed a Robinson script, *The Squealer*, before he left Paramount for Warners.[19] Although his first work for Warners in 1935 was negligible, Robinson hit his stride with *Captain Blood*, directed by Michael Curtiz. The studio's first swashbuckler, Errol Flynn's first starring role and his first of nine paired with Olivia De Haviland, *Captain Blood* was also Robinson's first hit picture. Richard Corliss claims Robinson was at his best with "romantics in spite of themselves: Bette Davis and Errol Flynn."[20] His writing of their dialogue gave them a sense of humor, a touch of self-criticism

18. Ibid.
19. Corliss, *Talking Pictures*, pp. 286–87.
20. Ibid., p. 289.

that allowed for detachment, accurately perceiving how others viewed them. "This ironic detachment kept their sense of destiny, of superiority, under control and allowed the moviegoer both to idolize and to identify with them."[21]

Casey Robinson made a major contribution to the development of Bette Davis's evolving screen personality. He wrote the scripts for five of her pictures in a six-year period when her screen personality was undergoing its biggest change; *Dark Victory, The Old Maid, All This and Heaven Too, Now, Voyager,* and *The Corn Is Green* occurred in peak years for Davis and offered a coherent character, both resilient and sympathetically self-sacrificing. Corliss argues that the strength of Robinson's narrative structuring and witty dialogue enabled him to present sentiment with "no false appeals to sympathy."[22] Tom Ryan similarly claims that Robinson's adventure films are stronger in their treatment of the personal relationships of their romantic protagonists than in their depiction of scenes of action.[23]

Robinson's own remarks on the architectural work of the screenwriter suggest the basis for some of the changes which he initiated in novel, Treatment, and screenplay. His reference to the "mistake" in the play version of *Dark Victory* is astute and applicable to his ideas for the first half of *Now, Voyager.* He claimed that having Judith Traherne's doctor announce in the ninth speech of *Dark Victory* that she is dying—before the audience meets and grows to love her—is as much a mistake as having Judith, at the end of the second act, announce to her horse trainer, Michael, that she has faced death, obviating the need for a third act.[24] So instead of having a transformed Charlotte presented at the very beginning of the film as Prouty does in the novel (relying on the immanent love affair to hold our interest for the flashback history and explanation), Robinson rejected both the novel's opening *and* that suggested by Goulding and began with Charlotte's

21. Ibid., p. 286.

22. Ibid., pp. 289–90.

23. Tom Ryan, Introduction to "Casey Robinson on *Dark Victory,*" *Australian Journal of Screen Theory,* 4:5.

24. Ibid., p. 6.

struggle against "the grim opposition" of her mother. He took his time in structuring the pleasure of the Cinderella story, which Prouty's image of the butterfly leaving its chrysalis suggested. Instead of presenting the suave-looking Charlotte embarking on her relationship with a married man, with numerous flashbacks and references to the past as explanations, Robinson included a single flashback, the traumatic enigma, but built our sympathy for Charlotte to a point where her affair is an assertive insistence on at least "the crumbs from the table."

This restructuring of the narrative and strengthening of Charlotte's will is crucial in repositioning the *mother-daughter relationship* as the terms of Charlotte's struggle and transformation. As Sam Rhode points out, the film opens and closes with a mother-daughter relationship: it opens with the rejection of Charlotte by her natural mother, to which Charlotte's illness can be attributed, and closes with Charlotte's accepting Jerry's child, Tina. The natural unwanted child becomes the accepting un-natural mother.[25] Jaquith and Jerry, a doubling of male father figures and lovers, are the means to Charlotte's becoming the adult parent of Tina and the mother she desired her mother to be. They become a means to an end rather than an end in itself, although Charlotte would have us believe that mothering Tina is her only access to Jerry and hence her motivation for becoming Tina's un-natural mother.

In some respects Prouty's novel lent itself easily to film script adaptation. It is a remarkably talky novel without the intricate and subtle governance of a narrating intelligence that provides insight, interpretations, and innuendo. Prouty claimed that her task was to allow her characters to speak and act plausibly. Easily three-quarters of the novel is conversation, and whether through Robinson's respect for the work of writers or Davis's insistence that the tone of the novel be retained, much of it is transposed directly into dialogue. Indeed critics who tend to praise Davis and Robinson for their wit knew little of how much

25. Sam Rhode, "Semiotic Constraints in *Now, Voyager,*" *Australian Journal of Screen Theory,* 4:21–22.

of that was supplied by Prouty's pen. What Robinson did do, however, was eliminate minor characters, drop the coincidences that have them intersecting, and reduce much of the conversation between Jerry and Charlotte. Robinson did achieve Goulding's call for "swift clean strokes" by condensing brief incidents into single scenes, eliminating the need for a whole scene by inserting the information into the conversation of another or using voice-over as memory to supply needed information. Interesting in light of the thesis that Prouty's is a novel of a woman's initiation into adult independence, the scenes between Charlotte and her mother are taken virtually intact from the novel. They contain important elements of character, like Charlotte's recognition of her mother's matriarchal strength as a positive quality ("Mother, there's no one like you") and her witty upbeat response to her mother's upbraiding challenge to her marital future ("I'll get a cat and a parrot and enjoy single blessedness").

The second part of the film script, which concerns Charlotte's mothering of Tina, changes the novel and early screenplay drafts, streamlining the narrative and making minor adjustments in dialogue and characterization. The film version, for example, does not have Charlotte and Tina changing a tire together on their camping trip. With Gladys Cooper/Mrs. Vale out of the film script during the second half and the rather cloying and clinging Tina occupying a good deal of screen time, Claude Rains's Jaquith assumes greater interest as the best match for the Davis persona in a field of enfeebled characters. Charlotte earns her peer professional relation with Jaquith by understanding the correct mothering for Tina. Although she asserts her judgment against his, Jaquith's "Go ahead. Maybe I'll like it" is still a giving of permission. Perhaps he *is* the good strong parent who encourages Charlotte's adulthood, but Charlotte has no opportunity to reciprocate Jaquith's role toward her. She explains to Jerry her lack of responsiveness to his romantic overtures with Jaquith's putting her "on probation." Being a good parent to Tina means, from Jaquith's point of view, the necessity of Charlotte's renouncing sexual interest in Tina's father. Despite her money for his sanitarium, her membership on the board, and her evolving credentials as a counsellor, Jaquith's ability to place her on probation maintains his patriarchal power. His pleasure in her assertiveness and the potential sexual excitement in the attraction of these strong-willed peers do not obliterate the power of his possible displeasure, which Charlotte does not have to face in this story.

Hays Office Influence

Although critics incorrectly attributed the Hays Office rather than the Prouty novel with the impossibility of two adulterers happily united at the end of the film, fear of censorship can plausibly account for some of the changes in the process of adaptation. Certainly the brevity of the scene between Jerry and Charlotte in their mountain cabin, cutting subtlely between the lovers and the diminishing fire, would be desired in a story already so blatantly challenging monogamy. In addition the film makes Charlotte older for her first romance with Leslie Trotter and Jerry's daughter Tina younger with, as yet, no interest in boys but an intense involvement with her father and Charlotte, which is more acceptable in a younger child. Prouty's Charlotte tells her fiancé, Elliot Livingston, that she fears she will be "frigid" with him and that he deserves not to have two frigid women in his life. Needless to say, this is left out of the film.

In the Revised Final, other objectionably explicit lines are dropped: in response to Elliot's "I did everything before I spoke to you," Charlotte's voice-over, "Except make love to me," is left out, as is her request that Elliot not stay the night after she has seen Jerry at the cocktail party and concert. Anticipation of Hays Office intervention may also have encouraged Robinson to drop the references in the novel and early script versions to Jerry's offering Charlotte whiskey from his thermos the night of their affair, although the Revised Final and film retain Charlotte's citing such behavior from a novel to Elliot, implying that she is disguising her own behavior. The "morning-after awkwardness" of the novel and Temporary disappears into a breezy conversation on a restaurant terrace about their week ahead together. The whole mountain cabin affair, like the romantic experience with Leslie Trotter, is reduced to conventional shorthand in the final film: shot of the mountain cabin, the fire, two lines about the sacred New England tradition of "bundling," shot of a dwindling fire, Jerry's "Sleeping Beauty" kiss of Charlotte. The awakening of "Sleeping Beauty" is evoked in the subsequent tearful scene: "No one ever called me darling before," which offers the passionate clinch of the film.

Influence of Psychoanalysis

Recent scholarship on the influence of psychoanalysis in American popular culture and Hollywood movies in particular suggests a topic of special interest in a discussion of *Now, Voyager*. The novel and film both deal explicitly with psychoanalysis insofar as Charlotte's nervous breakdown results in her getting psychotherapy and becoming engaged in helping someone else with what she has learned. Although Nathan C. Hale's study of popular psychoanalysis dates the 1909 Clark Conference as a significant point of entry for Freudian ideas into American thought, it is the second decade of the twentieth century that marks the extensive popularization of Freudian psychoanalysis with its discussion in mass circulation women's magazines, the first American psychoanalytic novel, and a wave of articles announcing that the most progressive, successful physicians were adopting Freud.[26] Nevertheless, film critics have noted that psychoanalytic themes did not become predominant in American cinema until the 1940s. When they did, however, it was through an emphasis similar to that of the teens on the cathartic method as the most popular image of psychotherapy. Marc Vernet has distinguished between the influence of Freud in a series of films that deals specifically with psychoanalysis almost as a genre and a more pervasive influence which integrated psychoanalysis into

26. Nathan G. Hale, Jr., *Freud and the Americans: the Beginnings of Psychoanalysis in the United States 1876 1917* (New York: Oxford University Press, 1971).

the narrative structure of Hollywood films: the presentation of an enigma traceable to trauma, the recurrence of the traumatic situation, the creation of a solution through recurrence, and a finale.[27]

Now, Voyager makes both explicit reference to psychoanalysis and incorporates the cathartic method into its narrative structure. It presents the trauma which "explains" a later enigma in the classic structural device Vernet cites: the flashback. Vernet does not claim that the flashback as a narrative device is attributable to the influence of psychoanalysis, but rather that, as the cathartic method became a basis of narrative structure in Hollywood films, the function of the flashback became increasingly identified with presenting the original trauma, which must be resolved and amended for the protagonist to be "cured" and the narrative resolved. Interestingly, the various stages from novel to film for *Now, Voyager* gradually reduce flashbacks to three, with the first and longest containing Charlotte's adolescent romance abruptly severed by her mother. Although several more flashbacks are presented in the novel and Temporary script, the Final script eliminates these fantasies, reminiscences, and alterations in linear order. *Now, Voyager* becomes the story of Cinderella transformed with a flashback explanation of the "rags" we find her in and a diversion of the romantic energy of her transformation into becoming a fairy godmother for someone else. The means of the transformation is, as Vernet describes, the recurrence of the original situation in which a trauma occurred but with the assertion of adult control and parental separation that allows Charlotte to undo the results of the first trauma.

The explicit influence of psychoanalysis is both denied and avowed by film adapters like Goulding, who disliked the role of psychiatry given in the book, "which understands so glibly such women and their restraints, longings and inhibitions."[28] Nevertheless, Goulding recognized the importance of the "sublima-

27. Marc Vernet, "Freud: Effets speciaux; Mise En Scene: U.S.A." *Communications*, 23 (1975):223–34.
28. Goulding, *Now, Voyager* Treatment.

tion" (his word) of Charlotte's sexual love of Jerry in raising his child. Casey Robinson's Final script walks a fine line between presenting the psychiatrist of the story as a powerful wise father opposed to the powerful bad mother (a structural relation which the only other two flashbacks of the film underline—compare figure 4 with figure 5 [pp. 42–43]) and, with specific dialogue, undercutting the image of psychiatry as intellectual puffery: Jaquith says he leaves analysis to the "fakers and writers of books"; Charlotte herself becomes a lay psychiatrist; Charlotte asks Trask if Jaquith is still handing out common sense as if it were medicine; Jaquith suggests his job is merely to serve as a road sign at his patient's intersection. But the film clearly presents psychoanalysis favorably in integrating it structurally, making it a means to Charlotte's growth, and foregrounding Rains, the psychiatrist, as a benevolent figure.

Now, Voyager, the Film

Variety listed *Now, Voyager* as Warner Brothers' fourth-highest top grossing film of 1942. Only eighteen films for that year did better financially industry-wide. Although *Mrs. Minniver* swept the Academy Awards for best picture, director, actress, supporting actress, screenplay, and cinematography—a fact that topicality rather than lasting critical acclaim seems to account for—Max Steiner won an Oscar for the music for *Now, Voyager,* and both Gladys Cooper and Bette Davis were nominated, Davis for the fourth time in four years after winning two Oscars for *Dangerous* (1935) and *Jezebel* (1938).[29] The fact that the January 1942 "Dollar Index of Marquee Values" indicates that Bette Davis was listed fifth of all Hollywood actors and actresses in power to sell tickets argues that the power of Davis's box office draw should be considered paramount in accounting for the film's popular success.[30]

29. Richard Shale, *Academy Awards* (New York: Ungar, 1978), pp. 48–50.
30. Bette Davis was listed as fifth from the top in the "Dollar Index of Marquee Values" (January 1942) in *Gallup Looks at the Movies* (American Institute of Public Opinion and Scholarly Resources, Wilmington, Delaware, 1979).

BETTE DAVIS

The opening of this essay suggested the importance of Bette Davis's contribution to *Now, Voyager*. Comments by Irving Rapper about Davis's participation in the direction of her films as well as countless critical commendations argue similarly for her presence as a major determinant. Indeed, Charles Affron's book, *Star Acting*, implies that the star in the case of Bette Davis must be considered an "auteur"—a controlling force in shaping the overall production.[31] One might argue that just as we are inclined to say, "That's an Alfred Hitchcock film," we similarly recognize a film as belonging to the *oeuvre* of Bette Davis. There are those who argue that she is among a handful of the greatest actors and actresses the American cinema has produced.

The attempts of the Hollywood studios to generate an image of glamor for their actresses has successfully buried the experience of work that many actresses shared in the film industry. The autobiographies of these women provide one form of documentation to counter the public's notion that it was an easy, overpaid living filled with romance, beautiful clothes, and expensive parties. Davis's autobiography enumerates the obstacles she fought in achieving a serious acting career: having to outperform while appearing to be a conventional woman in order to maintain social aceptance.[32] Like Olive Higgins Prouty, whose novel borrowed heavily from her personal experience, the strong self-sacrificing woman of Hollywood melodrama bore a striking resemblance to Davis's personal life. The clash of roles in Davis's life, were it made into a film, would make the role conflict Corliss noted in *Now, Voyager* pale by comparison. Davis's mother became the "wife" of the professional actress, while Davis felt she had to be father to her mother and sister after her own father left the family. At the same time she tried to be wife to a series of husbands who had to cope with the role of "Mr. Davis."

Davis was a contract studio actress forced into parts that were mediocre at best, disliked by male colleagues (Hal Wallis told

---

31. Charles Affron, *Star Acting: Gish, Garbo, Davis* (New York: Dutton, 1977).
32. Bette Davis, *The Lonely Life* (New York: Putnam, 1962), p. 158.

her he couldn't stand the kind of things she wanted to do in pictures, and Jack Warner described her in 1964 as "an explosive little broad with a sharp left")[33] and underpaid despite acknowledged power as a top box office draw.[34] In 1939 Davis's $4,000-a-week salary, which was *one third* of Paul Muni's or James Cagney's salary, made her the most highly paid contract actress at Warner Brothers.[35] Her experience made her a fighter or, in the language that was frequently used to describe her, a bitch. Davis's attempt to control her roles put her in the company of Cagney and Bogart; they shared among them about twenty suspensions from Warner Brothers for refusals of undistinguished roles. "Although my valid protestations prompted one savant to call me the Luther of Burbank, my bosses preferred the image of the unmanageable child,"[36] an image not attached to Cagney or Bogart.

But aside from the personal and professional experience Bette Davis brought to her role in *Now, Voyager* and the determination to participate in the direction and characterization of Charlotte Vale, she brought the results of an evolved persona as a star. Cathy Klaprat has documented the importance of the star persona as a chief means of film-product differentiation, and hence market stabilization, in the industry.[37] The machinery for evolving a star persona is box office grosses, fan mail, sneak previews, and exhibitor reaction. Despite the comparisons with the sex appeal of Slim Summerville,[38] Davis's first market label was a blond sex bomb, which, in 1934 with her fought-for role in *Of Human Bondage*, shifted to that of vamp. The vamp star image continued into the turning-point role in *Jezebel* (1938), which provided the transition from the blonde bitch vamp to the strong-

33. Jack L. Warner, *My First Hundred Years in Hollywood* (New York: Random House, 1965), p. 147.

34. *Gallup Looks at the Movies.*

35. James Silke, *Here's Looking at You, Kid* (Boston: Little, Brown, 1976), pp. 240–45.

36. Ibid., p. 245.

37. Cathy Klaprat, "The Star as Market Strategy," unpublished seminar paper, University of Wisconsin-Madison, 1979.

38. Sennett, *Warner Brothers Presents*, p. 126.

woman roles of *Dark Victory, The Old Maid,* and *Now, Voyager.* Combined with her films directed by William Wyler (*Jezebel, The Little Foxes,* and *The Letter*), these films expressed the tension of her persona as a strong woman who transgresses social conventions. Klaprat's research on the changing star persona also indicates how studio publicity and newspaper reportage followed these shifts, making the changing character seem to emerge from private life. The persona, however complexly evolved and originated, made its impact on narrative structure, setting determinations for action based on the psychological "realism" implied by characterization. This volume's Notes to the Screenplay, indicating the emendations and changes from Revised Final script to film, suggests changes that the Davis persona may have required. What Bette Davis/Charlotte Vale could or could not do in her role suggests a fascinating study in social construction of the person and persona.

The publicity which helped market *Now, Voyager* as a star vehicle for Bette Davis and made the film one of the outstanding box office successes of 1942 played upon Davis's ambivalence-inducing combination of strong self-sacrificing woman and vamp bitch, the elements of tension surrounding her basically transgressive character. Publicity presented Davis in a classic vamp pose with cigarette and the words, "Don't blame me for what happened." Reference to adultery is suggested by "It happens in the best of families," while "But you'd never think it could happen to her!" is written across a sedate Davis standing alone. A brush of dark color connects the Davis-Heinreid kiss in the poster with the first statement, while the second statement intersects the brushstroke but points to her standing alone. The Davis persona is the transgressor, not Heinreid/Jerry. At the same time her singularity, alone in her black velvet dress, suggests her strong-woman dimension with the hint of tragedy in her facial expression. This publicity contrasts strategy with the expression of petulant vamp that she wears in some of the other posters to reveal the ambivalence which Davis could inspire.

The pressbook for *Now, Voyager* suggests that this ambivalence provides attraction and spectator involvement: "Poll fans on Bette's plight, vote on whether or not Charlotte Vale violated society's code in bringing up the child of the man she loved, though she herself could not marry him."[39] The poll questioned whether Charlotte was right, whether she should rear Jerry's child, whether she should have married Elliot. Questions about the *affair* with Jerry, which the film poster implies and the film implies more strongly, aren't on the poll. But the trailer capitalizes on the sensational aspects of the innuendo—"I knew you were married. I knew what I was doing"—as well as the emotional climaxes of the mother daughter confrontation and the lovers. The trailer ends, "It's the most revealing story ever written about a woman from a girl aglow with the rapture of her first kiss to a woman fighting for the right to love."

THE DIRECTOR

Irving Rapper acknowledges that *Now, Voyager* was his first big film for Warner Brothers, and most commentators agree it is probably his best film. He had worked with Bette Davis before in *Kid Galahad* as assistant director to Michael Curtiz, whom he describes as his mentor but whom he seems to resemble very little. Rapper was particularly associated with Warner's biographical films, a genre along with "nonaction pictures" which Curtiz disdained and avoided. Rapper also worked with Davis as assistant director on *The Sisters* and *All This and Heaven Too*, which gave him standing as a creditable *metteur en scène*. He would later direct her in *The Corn Is Green*. Rapper's background was in the New York theater. He had attended New York University where he joined the Washington Square Players as stage director. He later appeared and directed on Broadway before coming to Hollywood where he first worked as assistant director and dialogue coach. In 1936 he became dialogue director at Warners, achieving his debut as full director in 1941. Some critics regard his work as betraying the staginess and talky direction of his theater work.

Rapper shared with Davis a reputation for rebelliousness as a

39. Pressbook for *Now, Voyager*, United Artists Collection, Record Group 1, Archives Division of the State Historical Society of Wisconsin, Madison, Wisconsin.

result of his policy of refusing nonliterate or trite scripts even though it meant going on suspension (ten times in seven years). Rapper was reluctant to take *Now, Voyager* because he had only a two-week respite from *The Gay Sisters* to prepare for it and his mother had recently died. Curtiz had already turned it down, and there is some sense that the contest of wills between Davis and her directors ("If a producer meddles in film direction, I have been a producer a long time") had much to do with this. Rapper refers to Bette Davis as "the greatest actress in the world" and claims she played a particularly involved role in the direction of her films. While he acknowledges her marvelously probing intelligence, which gave great strength to the director working with her, he also comments on one instance of disagreement in which he felt convinced he took the "correct" position. After he stewed for five days, she redid the scene on request. "You could get through to her," Rapper said later, "although she had enormous power at the studio."[40]

Davis claims in her autobiography that she worked to preserve the quality of Olive Higgins Prouty's novel, which at least one critic has predictably cited as a wrong-headed conviction. She writes: "I also used Miss Prouty's book and redid the screenplay in her words as we went along."[41] Rapper claims that when he was assigned *Now, Voyager* he was handed a finished script by Casey Robinson. If Davis had had a hand in the script construction, Rapper believes it must have occurred before he was assigned the project, but the screenplay versions themselves do not indicate Davis's work nor does the script from the film indicate significant deviations from the Revised Final screenplay. One wonders if, given Rapper's relative inexperience at full directorial control and Davis's box office clout and critical acclaim, Davis finally got her way in the scene in which Charlotte declares the terms under which she will stay in her mother's house. Davis delivers these lines while off-screen in a dressing room; the camera stays mostly on Gladys Cooper's back

40. Charles Higham and Joel Greenberg, *The Celluloid Muse: Hollywood Directors Speak* (New York: New American Library, 1969), pp. 225–32.
41. Davis, *The Lonely Life* p. 184.

and only occasionally her face. Davis had wanted to deliver the famous line in Wyler's *The Letter*—"I still love the man I killed"— with her back to her screen husband, Herbert Marshall, believing that the character could never say it to his face. Wyler disagreed and won, but resolved never to direct Davis again. The declaration of independence to the imperious Boston matriarch utilizes Davis's notion of "tempered indirection."

Rapper's direction is not highly individualized or idiosyncratic, and he discounted the value of the story of *Now, Voyager*, attributing the achievement of the film to "brilliant acting." Certainly the experience and professionalism of Claude Rains, Gladys Cooper, and Bette Davis dominated the film, their scenes providing the greatest excitement and energy. Rapper does claim credit for casting the film, explaining his choice of Ilka Chase and Bonita Granville as the "only people I can find who will needle Bette Davis."[42]

THE CAST AND CREW

Claude Rains and Gladys Cooper were indeed excellent veterans of the British stage and a good ensemble for Davis. Cooper, a chorine at sixteen and the foremost pin-up girl in Great Britain during World War I, achieved stardom in her twenties and managed London's Playhouse Theater. She appeared in occasional British silent films after 1914 but began her major screen career in Hollywood in 1940, after which she was nominated three times for an Academy Award. Rains began his film career in Hollywood in the 1930s at midlife after starting a career in acting as a child of eleven in Great Britain. He had a long career on the London stage before coming to the United States in 1926. After causing a sensation as the voice in *The Invisible Man* (1933), Rains became the quintessential suave character actor with a superbly controlled sardonic manner and great charm as hero or villain. He made very effective appearances opposite Bette Davis first in *Now, Voyager* and later in *Mr. Skeffington* and *Deception*. Rains never won an Academy Award although he was nominated four times. Cooper and Rains offered a suitable match for Davis. In-

42. Higham and Greenberg, *The Celluloid Muse*, p. 232.

deed, Davis's recent television roles suggest more than a little of Cooper's characterization of Mrs. Vale. The three of them provide the most memorable scenes in the film, which suffers somewhat when they are absent.

Paul Heinreid, who had worked with Otto Preminger in 1933 for Max Reinhardt's Vienna theater after a career in publishing, became an actor in England in 1935 and then in the United States in 1940. He is probably best known for his roles in *Now, Voyager* and *Casablanca*—the object of admiration of American women as a prototype of the Continental lover, aristocratic, elegant, gallant. He would appear again with Davis and Rains in *Deception*. Overshadowed in strength of personality by Rains and Cooper as well as Davis, Heinreid nevertheless gave a creditable performance as Charlotte's lover, though he was never nominated for an Academy Award nor listed among the Gallup Poll's "Dollar Index of Marquee Values."

If *Now, Voyager* bears any resemblance to the work of Michael Curtiz, it may be due to the work of Sol Polito, who worked as cinematographer. Although Ernie Haller was Davis's favorite cameraman (she tells the story of herself asking Haller why he couldn't make her as beautiful as he had in *Jezebel*, and he replied, "I'm not the cameraman I was seven years ago, Bette"), Rapper insisted on Polito, who had done twelve films for Curtiz from 1936 to 1942. Polito had been a cinematographer in Hollywood since 1918. Educated in New York City, Polito started as a publicity still photographer and became renowned for his fine black and white photography for Warner Brothers in the late 1930s and 1940s. He worked with Rapper on *Rhapsody in Blue* and with Davis in *The Petrified Forest* and then with both of them in *The Corn Is Green*. Polito's well-lighted cinematography had much to do with the pleasure of following Charlotte's transformation into an assertive and glamorous adult woman.

THE COMPOSER

Max Steiner, who won the only Academy Award *Now, Voyager* received—one of three Oscars in his career, although nominated for fifteen others—scored more than two hundred films mostly for RKO and Warners and was the doyen of Hollywood film composers. A Viennese-born composer and conductor, Steiner studied under Gustav Mahler and others at the Imperial Academy of Music in Vienna, completing the eight-year course in one year and graduating at the age of thirteen. At fourteen he wrote an operetta that ran for two years in Vienna, and at sixteen he became a professional conductor in England and at theaters in Paris. Arriving in the United States in 1914, Steiner conducted and orchestrated musical shows on Broadway, working with both Florence Ziegfield and Victor Herbert

In 1936 Kurt London listed Steiner with Newman and Forbstein as the most original musicians in Hollywood where, London argues, apart from the use of jazz in film, visual achievement generally exceeded musical.[43] John Huntley and Roger Manvell date the development of the symphonic style of musical scores with 1935 and Steiner's score for *The Informer*. Steiner claims that *The Informer* was the only instance in which as composer he was consulted by the scriptwriter about music prior to receiving the finished product. "We all won the Academy Award on that one," he writes. By 1935–36 the symphonic style of musical score had attracted the work of Prokofiev, Walton, Arthur Bliss, Britten, Thomson, Arthur Benjamin, and William Allwyn.[44]

Steiner believed that the composer was a member of a team. When the music is "star" it fails. "I have always tried to submerge myself,"[45] he writes. Yet the music for *Now, Voyager* has a good deal to do with the opulence of its sentiment without being excessively overbearing or repetitive. Indeed, Steiner found the most difficult aspect of film-scoring was to know where and when to have music.

THE FILM'S SIGNIFICANCE

The reviews of the film were mixed, usually citing some fine acting but despairing of the contrivances of plot that the entirely

43. Kurt London, *Film Music* (London: Faber and Faber, 1936), p. 212.
44. John Huntley and Roger Manvell, *The Technique of Film Music* (New York: Hastings House, 1957), p. 252.
45. Ibid.

male reviewers of *Now, Voyager* associated with this "women's film." In *Commonweal* Philip T. Hartung claimed that the film is so much like the "tripe dished up in women's magazines that it is difficult to imagine men having the patience to watch it through."[46] The *New York Times* claimed the story moves from a direct and commonsense dramatic treatment into a prudish fantasy and blamed the Hays Office or "its own spurious logic" for opening continually new vistas of neuroses. The *Times* praised Davis as the "young woman high-lighting her progress to emotional maturity with the decision and accuracy of an assured actress."[47] And this review perhaps best represents that coupling of the importance of the film to women while despairing of its lachrymose convolutions.

It is interesting that some three decades later a woman critic, Barbara Creed, would suggest in a scholarly film journal that, rather than the contortions required by the Hays Office (a responsibility which Prouty's novel belies), the Davis women's films share the requirement that a woman who violates social conventions suffer and resolve her conflict into a more socially acceptable role: from adultress to self-sacrificing mother and "spinster."[48] Creed's structuralist analysis argues that these narrative functions in women's melodrama, common as they are to the work of more than one authoress or film, say something about the society from which they emerge, not just the narrative idiosyncracies of Olive Higgins Prouty's fiction. The limitations, ritual rehearsal of values, and resolution of contradictions of "women's films" are the boundaries within which women must safely operate given women's social and cultural definition.[49]

By 1970 Richard Gertner and Martin Quigley, Jr. chose *Now, Voyager* as the representative selection for 1942 in *The Fifty Greatest Films,*[50] but in 1942 only Manny Farber responded to what

46. Philip T. Hartung, "*Now, Voyager,*" *Commonweal* (October 23, 1942):17.
47. Philip T. Hartung, "*Now, Voyager,*" *The New York Times* (October 23, 1942):25:3.
48. Barbara Creed, "Position of Women," pp. 27–31.
49. Ibid.
50. Richard Gertner and Martin Quigley, Jr., *Films in America, 1929–1969* (New York: Golden Press, 1970).

might be considered the film's greatest contribution. The appealing quality of the movie, he wrote, is the accuracy and extent to which it shows the relationship between a daughter and her mother. Writing for *New Republic*, Farber attributed the renunciatory and loftier happiness of the tragic-lady movie in this case to Prouty, not bothering to ask where Prouty might have gotten the idea.[51]

Now, Voyager fits comfortably within a tradition of the melodrama of female suffering and self-sacrifice. Thomas Elsaesser argues in "Tales of Sound and Fury" that bourgeois tragedies derived their dramatic force from the conflict between an extreme and highly individualized form of moral idealism in the heroes and a thoroughly corrupt yet seemingly omnipotent social class. ". . . The element of interiorisation and personalisation of what are primarily ideological conflicts, together with the metaphorical interpretation of class conflict as sexual exploitation and rape, is important in all subsequent forms of melodrama, including that of cinema."[52] Elsaesser argues then that the scenario of female suffering *symbolized* a position for the *bourgeoisie*, male and female alike. The melodrama of D. W. Griffith, such as the Little Dear One in *Intolerance* or the mother in *Way Down East*, exemplifies this ritual of female suffering.

Whether one agrees with Elsaesser's notion that the victimization of women—a political, economic, and physical reality—is significant as the *symbolic* representation of a class of *men* as well as women, it is apparent that by the 1930s and 1940s the suffering, self-sacrificing, and morally regenerative woman figures in a mode of address specifically aimed at women: the weepy, the sudser, the four-hanky movie.[53] The sanctity of *motherhood* is the mainstay of this genre. Despite attentions paid to heterosexual romance and the role of woman as male supporter, it is

---

51. Manny Farber, "*Now, Voyager*," *New Republic* 105 (November 2, 1942):577.

52. Thomas Elsaesser, "Tales of Sound and Fury," *Monogram*, 4:3.

53. Lea Jacobs, "Notes Towards a History of the Women's Film," unpublished seminar paper, University of California at Los Angeles, 1981. See also her article "*Now, Voyager*: Some Problems of Enunciation and Sexual Difference," *Camera Obscura*, 7 (Spring, 1981):89–104.

the value of positive, nurturing motherhood which is inviolable. Hence, the importance of Charlotte's struggle against the "bad mother" in *Now, Voyager* and the achievement of becoming the "good mother" for Tina as a doubling of herself.

Although the assertion of selfhood confronting the domineering parent is a central element of *Now, Voyager* in both novel and film, one cannot conclude that the story is in any way a denigration of motherhood or parenting, only that mothering can be perverse in its consequences rather than infallibly nurturing. "Dr. Jaquith says that tyranny is sometimes an expression of the maternal instinct. If that's a mother's love, I want no part of it. I didn't want to be born. You didn't want me to be born, either. It's been a calamity on both sides." What the story opposes is a mother's rejection of her child, her *failure* to love her child, her insistence on her own selfish emotional needs.

Charlotte's success at mothering Tina in the face of the failure of Mrs. Vale and Isobel confirms a fundamentally conservative position about women's roles and a reverence for motherhood which all versions of the script, film, and novel make explicit in these lines of Jaquith's: "Remember that whatever she may have done she's your mother." If Charlotte's memory slips, Jerry's does not. Having him remain loyal to his daughter's biological mother while giving Charlotte her greatest honor—referring to Tina as "our child"—allows the story to "have it both ways." Manny Farber praised that part of the film devoted to the struggle for a woman's adulthood:

. . . Cutting in and out of this silliness is the frank intelligence about dominating mothers. The interacting relationship of mother, daughter and psychiatry (which should have been the whole movie instead of a springboard for a frustrated love affair) is exceptionally accurate. The scenes in which average people are faced with a neurotic illustrate reactions and conversational responses which are emotionally exact. . . . The movie has fineness in spite of the distortion toward gentility given by its love affair.[54]

It should be added, however, that Farber's reference to Charlotte's mother as "a neurotic" accepts the terms which the film

54. Farber, *"Now, Voyager,"* p. 577.

as well as the novel to some degree set for responsibility within the framework of the story. Like recent movies such as *Ordinary People* and *Kramer v. Kramer, Now, Voyager* presents a mother as the villain of the melodrama, drawing a frame around her character that precluded a discussion of the patriarchal social systems which shaped and limited her options.[55] As Fina Bathrick has pointed out, the way the problem is defined and bracketed in these films determines its answer.[56]

But it may also be that the fought for maturity and independence which Charlotte Vale acquires in *Now, Voyager* shimmered on the screen luminously enough to withstand the convolutions of heterosexual romance and the circumstances of the melodrama's "bad mother." Molly Haskell suggests in her pioneering book, *From Reverence to Rape,* that although independent women had to be punished or made socially acceptable through submission (albeit romantically) to males, for a certain space and time they shone out strong, mature, and clear.[57] Bette Davis, with the support of Gladys Cooper and Claude Rains, gave us such a moment in *Now, Voyager.*

55. Mary Daly, *Gyn-ecology: The Mataethics of Radical Feminism* (Boston: Beacon Press, 1978), pp. 39–40 and passim.

56. Fina Bathrick, "*Ordinary People* and the Cult of True Womanhood," panel presentation at the Society for Cinema Studies Conference, New York City, April 22, 1981.

57. Molly Haskell, *From Reverence to Rape.*

1. The credits feature the ocean liner on which Charlotte Vale begins to transform her appearance and social status.

2. With these close-ups, the film conveys Charlotte's transformation from an oppressed, despondent daughter . . .

3. . . . to a more self-determining adult, discovering a new social world on shipboard.

4. Two flashbacks contrast Dr. Jaquith, the "good father," . . .

5. . . . and the "bad mother," Mrs. Vale, here represented in a superimposition over Charlotte's face as the presence Charlotte has gone abroad to escape.

6. Mrs. Vale interrupts Charlotte's tryst with Leslie Trotter and ends their romantic relationship.

7. *Charlotte's relationship with Jerry Durrance allows her to repeat and "correct" her previous romance.*

8. *Charlotte and Jerry compare family "photogravures" on shipboard. Notice the similarity in position and look of Jerry's daughter, Tina (far right) . . .*

9. . . . . and Charlotte (far right), both of them "unwanted" daughters.

10. Jerry and Charlotte "bundle" together in a mountain cabin and Jerry takes a courtly kiss from Charlotte's "Sleeping Beauty."

11. *At Jaquith's woodsy sanitarium Charlotte first mothers Tina, Jerry's daughter.*

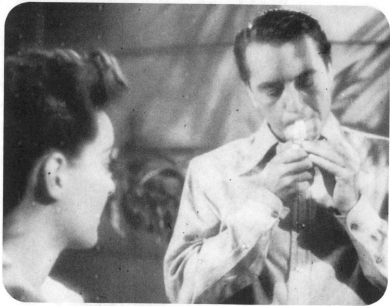

12. *Charlotte's romantic involvement with Jerry, popularly remembered in this ritual of lighting and sharing cigarettes, is an adulterous transgression . . .*

13. . . . . replaced by the nurturing mother-daughter relationship that "corrects" the childhood trauma of Charlotte's "bad mother."

14. Publicity featured Bette Davis as the strong and solitary woman who moves from a transgressing social position . . .

15. . . . *to a more conservative conventional one through self-sacrifice. Charlotte says goodbye to Jerry, her lover, and accepts her role as Tina's mother as her primary social identity.*

16. *Tina's first party dress and grown-up hair-do please her father, who answers her question, "Do you like me, father?"* . . .

17. . . . . with an embrace and a look directed to Charlotte: "I love you."

18. Charlotte's confrontation of her mother and her insistence on her privacy and independent decisions . . .

19. . . . is matched by Charlotte's assertiveness with Jaquith on the "proper care" of Tina.

20. The difference between Mrs. Vale's inability to accept Charlotte's separateness . . .

21. . . . . and Dr. Jaquith's encouragement of the adult Charlotte is evident in this visual opposition, although Jaquith's approval remains powerful.

22. The role of Ilka Chase (on Charlotte's left) as Charlotte's sister-in-law is considerably smaller in the film than in the novel.

23. Charlotte's shipboard "midwife," Deb, also has a smaller role.

Now, Voyager

Screenplay

by

CASEY ROBINSON

From a Novel

by

OLIVE HIGGINS PROUTY

Now, Voyager

FADE IN

1.   A BRASS PLAQUE BESIDE A DOORWAY

It bears a single word, a name:

        VALE

DISSOLVE TO:

2.   INT. VALE ENTRANCE HALLWAY

A GRANDFATHER CLOCK OF GREAT ANTIQUITY

Its hands point to a few minutes before 4 P.M.

PAN DOWN TO:

3.   AT THE FOOT OF THE MAIN STAIRWAY   WILLIAM

waits, looking up. Hilda, the parlor maid, and Katie, the upstairs maid, start through in background, giggling.

WILLIAM (with a sharp look at them):
    She's coming down.

His tone conveys both his authority over the maids and his awe toward the one "coming down." Instantly the girls stand at attention.

4.   MRS. VALE

comes down the staircase. She moves with a self-possessed dignity that is second nature. She does not seem to notice anyone but moves toward the drawing room. William follows.

MRS. VALE:
    We will probably be pouring tea in the drawing room this afternoon.

WILLIAM (off to maids):
 Hilda . . .

The maid designated bobs and disappears through a back hallway door. William follows Mrs. Vale into:

5. THE DRAWING ROOM
 It is a rich, solid, gloomy room. Over the fireplace, which never has a fire, there is a portrait of Mrs. Vale by Sargent. William hurries to hold her straight-backed wing chair for her as she continues.

MRS. VALE:
 Please ask Miss Charlotte to be down in ten minutes. (William bows. The clock out in the hallway strikes four.) My daughter-in-law, Mrs. Lisa Vale, is bringing someone at four o'clock. Show them in here. (There is a loud tapping sound from the hallway.) What's that noise?[1]

6. HALLWAY AT FRONT DOOR
 Lisa and Dr. Jaquith are just being let in by Hilda. He is knocking out his pipe against the edge of the door. As William enters from the drawing room and goes toward the door:

MRS. VALE'S VOICE:
 Whoever is doing that will kindly stop!

Dr. Jaquith is momentarily startled, then he grins at Lisa.

DR. JAQUITH:
 I imagine whoever said that—

LISA:
 Yes, that's Mother. I'll go ahead and smooth the path. (Exits.)

WILLIAM:
 This way, please.

Dr. Jaquith doesn't know what to do with the pipe ashes

he is holding in his hand. He looks about for an ashtray. There isn't one. William takes some calling cards off a silver tray and holds out the tray to Jaquith with a total lack of expression that is worse than a rebuke.

DR. JAQUITH:
Messy things, pipes. (Then, almost belligerently.) I like 'em.

HILDA (with a bob):
Your things, sir.

DR. JAQUITH:
Oh, yes—of course—

Divesting himself of his things, he follows William, feeling somewhat put in his place, half amused and half resentful of this. He inquisitively looks about the gloomily impressive hallway.

7.   PAN SHOT FROM DRAWING ROOM ENTRANCE
As William brings Jaquith along camera movement discloses Mrs. Vale and Lisa.

LISA (is saying):
But, darling, there can't be any possible harm in just talking—(She breaks off as she sees Jaquith.) This is Dr. Jaquith—My mother-in-law, Mrs. Henry Windle Vale.

DR. JAQUITH:
How do you do? (Camera follows him into the room.)

MRS. VALE:
I will not pretend, Dr. Jaquith, that you have been brought here with my approval. No matter what Lisa may have told you, my daughter Charlotte is no more ill than a moulting canary.

LISA:
That's what we hope he's come to confirm. (To Jaquith.) Mother's disapproval isn't personal, Doctor
. . .

MRS. VALE:

The last member of your profession I consulted warned me my heart would be the finish of me. The fact that I've outlived him fifteen years hasn't increased my meager trust of the pack of you.

DR. JAQUITH:
A highly sensible reaction.

LISA:

Well, darling, will you relax your gr-r-rim disapproval where *this* doctor is concerned? Really, dear, if you knew—We are having the honor of being visited by the foremost psychiatrist of the whole darn country. And I might add, he was pretty sweet to come all the way from New York to Boston. He doesn't come to people, they come to him.

DR. JAQUITH (with a twinkle):
It wouldn't hurt if you also added that that's from lack of time, not from vanity.

LISA:
Oh, and by the way, Mother, before I forget—Don't call him Dr. Jaquith in front of Charlotte.

MRS. VALE:
That's his name, isn't it?

LISA:

I mean the doctor part. Make him "mister." Charlotte will shut up like a clam if she suspects we've trapped her into an examination. So cooperate, old dear, will you?

MRS. VALE:
I have already sent for Charlotte. (To Jaquith.) My little girl will be down directly.

8.   CHARLOTTE'S DOORWAY   HALLWAY SIDE   WILLIAM

WILLIAM: (says as he knocks on the door):
Miss Charlotte—

9.   AT CHARLOTTE'S DESK   CLOSE SHOT   A PLATE
Instantly a cigarette is squashed out on it. There is a
lipstick stain on the tip of the cigarette. Then Charlotte's
hand, which has squashed out the cigarette, quickly
opens the desk drawer, takes out a piece of cleansing
tissue, and carries it up out of scene toward her lips.

WILLIAM'S VOICE:
    Your mother is waiting in the downstairs drawing
    room.

On this, Charlotte's hand comes into scene again. The
cleansing tissue is now smeared with lipstick hastily
wiped off. Charlotte clenches the tissue in her fist, then
she uses it to wipe off the plate, and, camera panning,
deposits the cigarette and the tissue in a scrap basket.

10. ON HER DESK   CLOSE SHOT   A BOOK
Her hands reach in and close it. We read the title: Boc-
caccio's *Decameron*. Camera pans with the book as Charlotte takes it to a bookcase. She pushes aside a hand-
tooled set of Ralph Waldo Emerson and hides the book
behind them. (Still, of course, we have seen nothing of
her but her hands.)

11. CHARLOTTE'S DOORWAY   HALLWAY SIDE   ONLY THE
     LOWER SIX INCHES
Sound of the door being unlocked. Charlotte comes out.
We see only her shoes, sensible low-heeled ones, nothing about them to indicate her age. She is heard to close
the door and lock it again and, camera moving ahead,
her feet cross the hall and start down the first flight of
stairs. In the middle of the flight there is a step that
creaks. As she reaches the first landing, where a door
leads into her mother's room, she stops as she hears
from downstairs:

MRS. VALE'S VOICE:

Is it facts about my daughter you want, or Lisa's fancies?

DR. JAQUITH'S VOICE:

Oh, just anything interesting. I always like to know a thing or two about people before I meet them. It makes talking easier.

Charlotte's feet move toward the second flight, camera preceding, and she starts down. This time, however, camera lets her step down more and more into shot, in other words, travels up her figure. Her dress is just a little too long to be fashionable, her figure is blocky, bulky, unconfined by restricting whalebone, uncontrolled by a restricting diet.

MRS. VALE'S VOICE:

Charlotte was a late child. There were three boys and then, after a long time, this girl. "The child of my old age," I have always called her—I was well into my forties, and her father passed on soon after she was born. My ugly duckling—Of course, it's true that all late children are marked . . .

DR. JAQUITH'S VOICE:

Often such children are not wanted. That can mark them.

MRS. VALE'S VOICE:

I've kept her close by me—always. When she was young, foolish, I made decisions for her—and always the right decisions. You would think a child would wish to repay a mother's love and kindness—(Her voice breaks, but by no means from any weakness of emotions.)

On this, camera reaches Charlotte's face. Actually Charlotte is twenty-eight, but judging from her face, she might be older, any age. Her hair is long and worn in a huge bun at the base of her head. Her expression is a stolid,

introverted mask. Her eyes, which are covered by rim-
less glasses, seem to have a curtain dropped in front of
them. (NOTE: For protection, also shoot above off-scene
dialogue as straight scene.)

12.   DRAWING ROOM
      as William brings in the tea table, assisted by Hilda. Ac-
      tually, the cut has taken place during Mrs. Vale's speech
      above and it is at the entrance of the servants that she
      has broken off speaking.

      MRS. VALE:
            In front of the couch, William. (Then, catching sight
            of Charlotte as latter approaches.) There you are,
            Charlotte. Just in time.

      LISA (hurries to her):
            Charlotte, dear! I'm awfully glad to see you.

      She kisses Charlotte's cheek. Charlotte smiles. She likes
      Lisa. Then Charlotte sees the stranger in the room and
      her expression freezes just a little.

      LISA:
            Oh—this is my very good friend, Mr. Jaquith.

      DR. JAQUITH:
            How do you do, Miss Vale?

      Dr. Jaquith has risen. If the sight of Charlotte has been
      a shock to him, he has well concealed it. There is prac-
      tically no response from Charlotte, only the slightest in-
      dication of a nod.

      MRS. VALE:
            You will pour, Charlotte.

      William and Hilda exit. Charlotte moves obediently to
      the couch behind the tea table. Whatever she may be
      feeling or thinking is impossible to know, for her face is
      inscrutable. She leaves the burden of making conversa-
      tion to the others.

LISA:

> I just happened to run into Mr. Jaquith on the street, so I brought him by for tea. I knew Mother would be delighted, and I hoped you would be, too. (She pauses for a fraction, but there is no response.)

MRS. VALE (to Charlotte):
> Well, has the cat got your tongue?

Charlotte looks at her. The veil suddenly lifts from her eyes, and for a moment the utmost hatred shows in them. Mrs. Vale does not miss it. (Interchange close-ups.) She looks back at Charlotte and then she turns to Dr. Jaquith and speaks with the utmost deliberation.

> I apologize for the bad manners of my daughter— Doctor.

LISA:
> Mother!

MRS. VALE (to Lisa):
> I will not countenance deceit, Lisa, against one of my own flesh and blood. But neither will I countenance any more of Charlotte's nonsense. (To Charlotte.) Lisa says that your recent peculiarities—your fits of crying, your secretiveness—indicate that you are on the verge of a nervous breakdown. Is that what you are trying to achieve?

Charlotte is looking about at them, like a trapped animal, defiantly.

LISA:
> Charlotte, dear, I meant to help.

MRS. VALE:
> Dr. Jaquith has a sanitarium—in Vermont, I believe. Probably one of those places with a high wire fence and yowling inmates. Is that the sort of home you would be proud to trade for your own?

DR. JAQUITH (easily but firmly):
Well, now, I wouldn't want anyone to have that mis-taken notion. Cascade is just a place in the country. People come there when they're tired. You go to the seashore—they come there.

MRS. VALE:
The very word "psychiatry," Dr. Jaquith—(To Char-lotte.) Can it be that it does not fill you with shame—my daughter—a member of our family—

DR. JAQUITH (interrupts):
There's nothing shameful in my work—or frighten-ing, or anything else. It's very simple, really, what I try to do. (A quiet, direct appeal to Charlotte.) People walk along a road. They come to a fork in the road. They are confused, they don't know which way to take. I just put up a signpost: not that way, this way.

MRS. VALE (to Charlotte):
Now, if we can all resume a more seemly manner.

But Charlotte, visibly shaken, just turns and walks out of the room.

LISA:
Really, Mother—

DR. JAQUITH:
Excuse me. (Exits after Charlotte, calling.) Miss Vale, please wait.

13.   HALLWAY   THE TWO
Charlotte stops at the foot of the stairs. Dr. Jaquith joins her.

DR. JAQUITH:
I wonder if I might ask you a favor? Will you be nice enough to show me around this house? One doesn't often get the chance . . . (Charlotte just shakes her head and starts upstairs. He follows right after,

making it a joke.) That's right. I had a look at the *downstairs* when I came in.

14.   ANGLE DOWN FROM FIRST LANDING

DR. JAQUITH (heartily):
By gad, there's nothing like these old Boston homes anywhere. Here on Marlborough Street or on Beacon Hill you see them standing, firm, in a row like bastions, proud, resisting the new. Houses turned in upon themselves, hugging their pride.

CHARLOTTE (with bitterest mockery):
Introverted, Doctor?

DR. JAQUITH:
Eh? (He looks at her in surprise but she says nothing more.) Well, I wouldn't know. I don't put much faith in scientific terms. I leave them to the fakers and the writers of books.

They come up the last few steps in silence. Charlotte opens a door on the first landing, but doesn't go inside.

CHARLOTTE (with mocking self-contempt):
Now here is the room in which I was born. My mother's room. You may look at it if you like.

Dr. Jaquith steps past her into the doorway and for a moment looks around the room.

DR. JAQUITH:
It's a fine room.

CHARLOTTE:
Do you think so?

DR. JAQUITH:
Of course, I'd rather see what your room is like. Is it nearby?

CHARLOTTE:
I'm not your patient yet, Doctor.

DR. JAQUITH:
> Well, now, nobody thinks you ever will be. (His eyes twinkle.) I've seen the rooms of a lot of people who aren't my patients. My friends. I had hoped that you and I— Of course, if you'd rather not . . .

For a moment she looks at him with hostile challenge, but she can't find any answering challenge in his look, only an open friendliness. One corner of her mouth is lifted with a wry smile.

CHARLOTTE:
> It's on the floor above. (She goes up the second flight of stairs. He follows.)

15.   AN ANGLE FROM THE FLOOR ABOVE
They come up in silence until she steps on the squeaky tread, and a step behind he does, too.

CHARLOTTE:
> When I was seventeen I stayed out once until after midnight. That tread hasn't been fixed since.

Dr. Jaquith chuckles. When they reach the landing outside her door, Charlotte hesitates, remembering that the door is locked. Then, with a defiant gesture, she takes out her key and unlocks it.

CHARLOTTE:
> She locks her door. Make a note of it, Doctor. Significant, is it not?

DR. JAQUITH:
> Well, it signifies it's your door. I've never heard it said that a woman's home is not her castle.

She swings the door open and walks in ahead of him.

CHARLOTTE:
> My castle, Doctor.

16.   INT. CHARLOTTE'S ROOM
as he follows her in. Most of the articles in the room
have been selected by Charlotte's mother. A "set" of ma-
hogany furniture—a swell-front bureau and a swell-front
chiffonier, two chairs, and twin beds. Over the marble
mantel by the fireplace, a photogravure of the Coliseum
by moonlight; over a marble-topped table, another photogravure of the pigeons in St. Mark's Square. There is
also an engraving of a woman with long, crimpy hair,
kneeling before a cross, and several of Aunt Lizzie's wa-
tercolors of Gloucester sea-scenes in narrow gold frames.

In its furnishing the room is divided clearly into two
parts, half bedroom, half living room. In the living half,
besides the fireplace, there is Charlotte's desk. And there
is also a workbench, complete with a set of tools for
carving ivory. On the bench there is some raw ivory and
a half-finished figurine. Above it, on a shelf, are some
finished products, figurines and boxes, exquisite in design and professional in execution.

Charlotte is waiting for the first smile of amusement
to show on his face, but no such smile shows.

DR. JAQUITH:
You're comfortable here.

CHARLOTTE:
I try to be. I'm here a good part of the time.

He taps his palm against the top of the bureau, rubs the
wood to feel its finish.

DR. JAQUITH:
Stuff like this was built to last a liftime. It's solid.

CHARLOTTE:
Enduring, and inescapable.

DR. JAQUITH:
Hello, what's this? (He walks over to the workbench. It is difficult to tell if he has just noted it or
whether he has deliberately changed the subject—

66

put up one of those mental signposts of his, saying "Not that way, this way.") Did you do these?

CHARLOTTE:
Why shouldn't I?

DR. JAQUITH:
The point is how you could. They're really professional. Do you mind if I take a look at them?

His enthusiasm is so genuine that for the first time she unbends.

CHARLOTTE:
No, I don't mind. (She crosses to the workbench.)

17.   CLOSER ANGLE   TWO   AT WORKBENCH

CHARLOTTE:
They aren't difficult. I buy the raw ivory from New York. I have the tools. It only takes the doing.

DR. JAQUITH:
And the skill. That's really good detail. I have a very real admiration for people who are clever with their hands. I was always clumsy with my own.

CHARLOTTE:
I would say that you are one of the least clumsy persons I have every known.

For the moment her constraint seems to have dropped away entirely, and the look she gives him is sincere and friendly and somehow appealing. He smiles back at her. Then, as if her display has been embarrassing to her, she drops her eyes.

CHARLOTTE (carelessly):
You may have one of them if you like.

DR. JAQUITH:
May I, really? Any one?

CHARLOTTE:

Of course. (Then, as he reaches for a box.) Except that one. I spoiled that one. (Takes it down.) See, there's a gash across the top of it.

DR. JAQUITH (fingers the mark):

A slip, I suppose.

CHARLOTTE (with a bitter smile):

When I was carving it, I suddenly thought of my mother. I saw her face in front of me and I *dug* the chisel right into the bone.

DR. JAQUITH:

A pity to have ruined a nice box.

CHARLOTTE:

If it's boxes you like, this should do. (Gets him another.)

DR. JAQUITH:

Thank you very much.

CHARLOTTE:

I'll get you something to wrap it in.

DR. JAQUITH:

Don't bother.

18.   AT DESK   CHARLOTTE

enters. As she is about to open a drawer, she sees an old leather-bound portfolio lying on the desk. With what almost amounts to a guilty backward glance, she snatches it up.

CHARLOTTE:

No trouble. (And opens the drawer.)

19.   DR. JAQUITH

DR. JAQUITH:

Just any old piece of paper, then.

He glances down at:

20.   INSERT   THE SCRAP BASKET
with the lipstick-marked cleansing tissue and cigarette stub clearly visible.

21.   DR. JAQUITH
notes them, looks off at her.

22.   THE TWO   FROM DESK
Charlotte has taken out some paper and is about to put the book in the drawer. Dr. Jaquith taps his coat pockets.

DR. JAQUITH:
You wouldn't happen to have a cigarette hidden away someplace? (Charlotte freezes. For a moment she says nothing, but her every muscle is taut.) I seem to have left my tobacco in my coat downstairs.

CHARLOTTE:
Do you think I hide cigarettes in my room, Doctor?

DR. JAQUITH:
No, no—

CHARLOTTE:
Where do I hide them, Doctor? On the shelves behind the books? (She is actually trembling.) Cigarettes and medicated sherry and the books my mother would never allow me to read? A whole secret life hidden up here behind a locked door?

DR. JAQUITH:
Please. It was only the box that reminded me.

CHARLOTTE:
How very perceiving you are, Doctor. How very right you are. And see, I was about to hide this album. (With camera following, she goes back to him and tosses the album onto the workbench.) You really should read it. It wouldn't do for you to have come all the way up here and missed your amusement.

Read it, Doctor—the intimate journal of Miss Charlotte Vale, spinster.

DR. JAQUITH:
Won't anything convince you that I don't wish to
pry?

CHARLOTTE:
But you must pry. I insist that you do. (Opens the
book and begins turning pages.) There is really
nothing to frighten you off. A few snapshots, a me-
mento or two. It's only the record of my last trip
abroad. With my mother. There's our ship, a P and
O steamer. We were sailing up the coast of Africa.
You wouldn't have known me then. I was *twenty* then!
ABRUPTLY CAMERA SWINGS AWAY INTO A BLUR,
                                THEN SWINGS RIGHT BACK INTO:

23.   UPPER DECK OF STEAMER   CLOSE SHOT
       CHARLOTTE AND YOUNG MAN
embracing. Their kiss is long and almost shockingly
passionate—on her part especially—for she is young and
in the throes of first love. He wears the white uniform
of a ship's officer, and the cap that is pushed back on his
head identifies him as the radio officer. This is Leslie
Trotter. The two are hidden in a corner by a lifeboat.
When they finally break:

LESLIE (almost with a whistle):
I say! That *was* a scorcher.

CHARLOTTE:
You always act so funny, Leslie. Do I—? I thought
that men didn't like girls who were prudes.

LESLIE:
You're gorgeous, Charlotte. (Then with a start.) Eyes
open. There's the first mate. He'll be looking for me.
There's always a mess of work just before we dock.

CHARLOTTE:
Are you going ashore tonight?

LESLIE:

    Are we, pet?

CHARLOTTE:

    Darling, if I can't, then you won't either, will you?
    Even if that girl from New York does?

LESLIE:

    Not likely. There's nothing like you to be found in
    Africa. There he is again. I'd better hop it. (He starts
    away.)

CHARLOTTE:

    Leslie!

LESLIE:

    What? (Turns back.)

CHARLOTTE (kisses a fingertip and puts it on his lips):

    Darling . . . Dearest darling . . .

He winks at her and exits. She stands hugging herself
for an instant. (Hold this long enough for following dialogue.)

CHARLOTTE'S VOICE (speaking bitterly, intensely):

    I had read that part in novels— about men not liking
    girls to be prudes. That's all I had to go by, novels.
    Leslie told me he'd rather have me than any girl on
    board, or any girl he'd ever known, because I was
    so responsive. He said that the others were like silly
    schoolgirls compared to my warm, generous love-
    making.

Her words carry over the

                                          DISSOLVE TO:

24.   INT. SHIP'S WRITING ROOM   MRS. VALE
     is writing a letter at a desk in foreground. She moves
     her pen rapidly and with authority. Charlotte looks in at
     the door. She is carrying her bag and a book. Seeing her
     mother, she comes to her and looks down upon her

mother's head bent over the letter. Her strict training shows, because she does not immediately speak, but waits for her mother's head to come up, almost irritably, at the feeling of her presence.

MRS. VALE:

Why aren't you wearing your glasses?

CHARLOTTE:

They're in my bag. (Opens her bag; then.) Mother, they're so unattractive. Other girls—

MRS. VALE:

You'll never get another pair of eyes, my dear. What is that book?

CHARLOTTE:

Marconi—wireless—I'm learning about it.

She puts the book on the writing desk. She puts on her glasses—the horn-rimmed type—but she takes her time about putting them on. There is a pause. Mrs. Vale looks at the book, then at her daughter. Then she turns squarely around.

MRS. VALE:

From whom are you learning about wireless?

CHARLOTTE:

Mr. Trotter lent me this.

MRS. VALE:

You mean the wireless officer?

CHARLOTTE:

Mother, are we taking the shore trip tonight? I just met the ship's hostess and she asked me . . .

MRS. VALE:

No, Charlotte, I think not.

CHARLOTTE:
> Then I can go alone? Oh, not really alone. She said
> they're organizing groups and I said I'd ask you . . .

Mrs. Vale looks down at her letter as if the subject were
beyond discussion. Then she speaks without looking up.

MRS. VALE:
> Could we try to remember we are hardly commer-
> cial travelers? Charlotte, it's plain you don't realize
> the things you can pick up in these dirty African
> towns.

CHARLOTTE:
> But we've *stayed* on this ship . . .

MRS. VALE (looks up suddenly, almost violently):
> Sit down, Charlotte, at once. A quarrel would be
> most unpleasant, but— (She raps the desk with solid
> anger.) For the last three days you have been behav-
> ing like an excited servant girl! I have said nothing,
> but—

CHARLOTTE (showing plainly her fear at the rising tide
of her mother's anger):
> Please, Mother . . . Yes, I know—Don't go on, please
> . . .

MRS. VALE:
> One would almost think you did it on purpose to
> upset me—as if the heat wasn't enough . . .
>> DISSOLVE TO:

25.   STOCK SHOT   THE SHIP   NIGHT
tied up at dock. Tropical moonlight, distant music, atmosphere, etc

CHARLOTTE'S VOICE (with bitter intensity):
> That night I left her in her room with one of her
> headaches. I would go to the library and read. Later,
> when she looked for me, I wasn't there. She couldn't

know I was with Leslie—but she knew I hadn't gone ashore—she'd checked on that.

DISSOLVE TO:

26.   FREIGHT DECK   AT BOW OF SHIP
Camera is moving forward, following the rays from a flashlight which is being waved about among the pile of crates and canvas-covered automobiles.

CHARLOTTE'S VOICE (continuing):
Leslie and I always had to be discreet—not only to thwart mother's keen eyesight but because of his position on the ship as well. One of our favorite trysting places was on the freight deck among the crates and canvas-covered automobiles. There was a particular limousine—

Suddenly the flashlight goes over an object on the deck and then swiftly jumps back to it and stops. Camera stops. Lying on the deck near the slightly ajar door of the canvas-shrouded car are Charlotte's bag and her horn-rimmed spectacles.

CHARLOTTE'S VOICE (continuing; mockingly):
That was once I *should* have worn my glasses.

Mrs. Vale and the ship's captain walk forward into shot directly to the car's door. Mrs. Vale swings the door open and the captain sends the beam of the flashlight piercing into the interior. There is a startled half-gasp from inside.

MRS. VALE:
Come out at once!

CAPTAIN (ordering):
Trotter!

The two scramble out of the car. Charlotte faces her mother defiantly.

CHARLOTTE:
I don't care! I'm *glad!*

74

MRS. VALE:
>Go to your cabin.

LESLIE:
>I want to marry your daughter. We're engaged to be married.

MRS. VALE (to the captain):
>Do you allow what you call your officers to address a passenger in that manner?

CAPTAIN:
>You will report to my quarters at once, Trotter.

Charlotte walks away, camera panning with her. Her head is high.

CHARLOTTE'S VOICE:
>I had said I was glad—and I *was* glad. He had defied my mother and placed me upon a throne—and before a witness, too! It was the proudest moment of my life![2]

DISSOLVE TO:

27.   INT. CHARLOTTE'S BEDROOM   CLOSE SHOT   CHARLOTTE is seated at her desk. Her head is high. Her proud look bridges the years from the fresh young girl of twenty to the present-day Charlotte. But only for a moment does her look remain so. It changes—first to the acute pain of disillusionment, second, to the acute bitterness of resentment. Camera pulls back to include Dr. Jaquith. He is fiddling with his pipe and listening calmly, as one might listen to a story from a book.

CHARLOTTE (bitterly and with self-scorn):
>My moment did not last long, as you may guess. *She* smashed it. Leslie was not suitable—for a Vale of Boston. What man is suitable, Doctor? She's never found one. What man would come along and look at me and say, "I want you"? I am fat. My mother disapproves of the folderols of diet. I wear these

75

shoes—(She shows them.) My mother approves of *sensible* shoes. Regard the books on my shelves. My mother approves of good, solid books. I am my mother's well-loved daughter. I am her companion. I am her servant. My mother says— (With sudden hysterical violence.) My mother—my mother—my mother!

Then, as suddenly, she breaks. She sobs with her head on her arms on the desk. It cannot be said that Dr. Jaquith's expression shows one ounce of sympathy. He walks to her and picks up her glasses that she has brushed off as her head has gone forward.

DR. JAQUITH:
You'll never get another pair of eyes—as your mother says. If you spoil them with tears—

CHARLOTTE (looks up with sudden pleading):
Dr. Jaquith, *can* you help me!

DR. JAQUITH:
Help you?

CHARLOTTE:
When you were talking downstairs—when you talked abou the fork in the road—There are other forks further along the road—so many—

DR. JAQUITH (firmly):
You don't need my help. (She is shocked. Starts to speak again, but doesn't.) Put away your book and wipe off your eyeglasses and come downstairs. I'll go ahead. Thank you again for this. (He picks up the ivory box and walks out.)

WIPE OFF TO:

28.   INT. DRAWING ROOM   GROUP
as Dr. Jaquith comes back into the room.

MRS. VALE:
Your tea is getting too strong. Well, it's what I said, isn't it? Just nonsense?

DR. JAQUITH:
She is most seriously ill.

MRS. VALE:
Charlotte is—

DR. JAQUITH:
Thanks to you.

MRS. VALE:
Did you say—

DR. JAQUITH:
My dear Mrs. Vale, if you had deliberately and maliciously planned to destroy your daughter's life, you couldn't have done it more completely.

MRS. VALE:
How? By having exercised a mother's rights?

DR. JAQUITH:
A mother's rights, twaddle. A child has rights. A person has rights—to discover her own mistakes, to make her own way, to grow and blossom in her own particular soil.

MRS. VALE:
Are we getting into botany, Doctor? Are we flowers?

They break off at the sound of chatter from the hallway.

29. HALLWAY AT FRONT DOOR
William is just letting in Lisa's daughter, June. Here is a fresh, gay note, saucy, sixteen.

JUNE (is saying):
Hello, William, gloomy William.

WILLIAM:
Good afternoon, Miss June.

JUNE (looking at his head):
> William, I've been thinking you should get yourself a toppiece such as Mrs. Vincent Adams has put on her Charles.

WILLIAM:
> It is a project worth considering. I myself have been worried . . .

JUNE:
> Black, I think—or maybe red—Let's give it some thought—(Exits.)

30.   FOOT OF STAIRS   CHARLOTTE
is just coming down. June bounces in.

JUNE:
> Aunt Charlotte, you look ravishing. A new dress? (Of course she is joking. "Ragging Aunt Charlotte" is her favorite game.)

CHARLOTTE:
> No, June.

JUNE:
> Anyway, it's devastating. But do you think that even at our age we should wear our skirts so short?

LISA (from the drawing room):
> Mind your manners, June.

They go into the drawing room. Charlotte is making every effort to control herself. The scene upstairs has unnerved her to a dangerous point.

31.   INT. DRAWING ROOM   GROUP

MRS. VALE:
> We're still waiting for our tea.

JUNE:
> Hi, Grandma. No tea for me—I'm heading out for cocktails later. (Notices Jaquith.) Who's this?

LISA:

> *This* is Doctor Jaquith.

JUNE:

> And I'm June. You've heard about us —(A hug for Lisa.) June and December.

LISA (with a "face"):

> My Infant.

JUNE (spies the box):

> What's that? Don't tell me Charlotte gave you that? One of her precious, private . . . (Turns to Charlotte.) Aunt Charlotte, 'fess up. A romance? Isn't this something that should be discussed with your family?

Charlotte is trying to pour a cup of tea, but her hand shakes so that some of the tea spills.

MRS. VALE:

> Can't you pour a cup of tea? At my age I can pour tea. (Takes the pot from her.)

JUNE:

> What's this, old dear? A hangover? I believe it is. Aunt Charlotte's got the shakes!

Then it happens, a sudden, complete collapse. Dry sobs shake Charlotte's whole frame.

CHARLOTTE:

> Do you enjoy being disagreeable? Do you get pleasure out of making others uncomfortable? Do you—[3]

Her voice is shut off by a flood of rising sobs. She puts her hands to her mouth to choke off the awful sound they make. Everybody turns to stare at her. She blindly makes her way out of the room and runs upstairs.

LISA (sharply to June):

> Nice work. (She hurries after Charlotte.)

JUNE:
>   I didn't mean—why, we've always ragged Aunt
>   Charlotte. It was a game.

She stops when she finds out that nobody is listening
to her. Mrs. Vale has risen and is looking out toward the
doorway, her dignity outraged that a member of her
family should have created such a scene, and Dr. Jaquith is looking at Mrs. Vale. She catches his look, and
if at first she is a little frightened, she finally replies with
a look of haughty defiance.

MRS. VALE:
>   A nervous breakdown! No member of the Vale fam-
>   ily has ever had a nervous breakdown.

DR. JAQUITH:
>   Well, there's one having one now. I suggest a few
>   weeks at Cascade.

>   DISSOLVE TO:

32.   EXTREMELY LONG SHOT   THE WHOLE OF CASCADE
It is as Dr. Jaquith described it, a secluded spot in the
country with two identical farmhouses on a hill. One is
called Oldways and was built in 1825, the other New-
ways and was built in 1925. They are charming, homey
houses and are connected by a woodshed. To one side
there is a huge red barn, and behind it there are apple
orchards, hayfields, pastures, stone walls, and acres of
woods.

>   DISSOLVE TO:

33.   EXT. CASCADE
In foreground Dr. Jaquith is waiting as in background
Lisa gets out of her car and hurries to him.

DR. JAQUITH (heartily):
>   Well, well, Lisa, here you are! Lovely as ever, I see.
>   It's good to see you again.

LISA:

> A little late. I'm sorry. I lost my way. How's Charlotte?

Camera trucking ahead, they walk toward one of the cottages. Background action shows some people on the tennis court, others at archery, other patients taking a walk—good, healthy, happy atmosphere.

DR. JAQUITH:

> Better every week. In fact, almost well. But she doesn't believe it. The prospect still looks dark to her. (Pauses reflectively.) Going through a sickness like hers is something like going through a tunnel— pretty dark right up to the last few hundred yards. You'll find her feeling depressed today, as I've told her just this morning she's a fledgling now.

LISA:

> A fledgling?

DR. JAQUITH:

> Yes. The time has come for her to get out of the nest and try her own wings. The contemplation of going home has struck her pretty hard. I haven't told her yet there is any alternative.

LISA (eagerly):

> You think well of my alternative?

DR. JAQUITH:

> Think well of it! It's a gift from heaven. We won't tell her your plan for her until after you've gone. I think. (Pauses at cottage door.) You mustn't expect to see her looking very well. She's lost a lot of weight, you know. She's been a very sick girl, remember.

34. INT. CHARLOTTE'S ROOM

It is a small, simple room. Charlotte is seated in an armchair. Beside her, in another chair, is Miss Trask, the head nurse. Miss Trask is helping Charlotte with some weaving on a handloom. As Dr. Jaquith and Lisa come in, Miss Trask stands up. Charlotte has indeed lost weight, and there is definitely a disintegration to be noticed in her, the result of the complete collapse of her last vestiges of fight. She is just listless. She just doesn't care. She sits staring dumbly at the brilliantly lovely Lisa, her old clothes hanging loosely on her figure, her hair drawn straight back from her gaunt features in its accustomed bun. Lisa immediately crosses the room, puts her arm around her, and kisses her warmly.

LISA:
Hello, Charlotte! Dr. Jaquith says you're much better—almost well!

CHARLOTTE:
Yes. That's what he *says*.

DR. JAQUITH:
Lisa, this is Miss Trask. Mrs. Vale. Miss Trask is the chief of my police force here. We couldn't run the place without Miss Trask. (Notices the weaving.) What's this?

MISS TRASK:
I was helping Miss Vale with her weaving. Now you've come, if you'll excuse me, I've a million things to do. (Exits.)

During the above Charlotte has nervously put on her glasses as she, too, looks at the weaving.

DR. JAQUITH:
The optometrist told you you don't need these anymore. (Takes them off her.)

CHARLOTTE (reaching for them):
I feel undressed without them.

DR. JAQUITH:
Good for you to feel that way.

He snaps the glasses in two and puts the broken pieces

in his pocket. In the somewhat uncomfortable pause
which follows, Lisa inspects the weaving.

LISA:
> Isn't this lovely. Did you weave it, Charlotte?

CHARLOTTE (ignoring the question):
> How's Mother?

LISA:
> Oh, she's fine. Really having a marvelous time pay-
> ing visits to all her children. Spending a month with
> me now.

CHARLOTTE:
> Has Dr. Jaquith told you?

LISA:
> Told me what?

CHARLOTTE (with despair):
> He says I'm well enough to leave here now. I've got
> to go home. Lisa—I dread it terribly. It's awful, I
> suppose, not to want to go home and be with Mother.
> It's wrong, I suppose—but—

DR. JAQUITH (amused):
> Stop, look, and listen! New England conscience on
> the track.

LISA:
> Perhaps you won't have to go home. (To Dr. Jaquith
> eagerly.) Mayn't I tell her?

DR. JAQUITH:
> Later, maybe. We'll see how she behaves. (Then to
> Charlotte with a mischievous wink.) We have a
> scheme, your relative and I.

CHARLOTTE (without much interest):
> What is it?

DR. JAQUITH:

> I'm not telling you yet. It's a marvelous chance, though, to use your "reeducation." (Takes out watch and looks at it.) My time for pleasure is about over. (To Charlotte.) I thought I'd show Lisa around the place a little. Then you can show her the rest of the works when we get back. (To Lisa.) Meet me outside in a minute.

LISA (taking the hint):

> Oh, I've been thrown out of lots of places. (Exits.)

Alone with Charlotte, Dr. Jaquith reaches into his pocket and takes out a slip of paper from his billfold.

DR. JAQUITH (slowly and gravely):

> This morning, Charlotte, during your office appointment with me, I referred to a quotation. Remember?

CHARLOTTE (vaguely):

> You said it was from Walt Whitman but you couldn't quote it.

DR. JAQUITH:

> That's right. Well, I've had it looked up and typed for you on a slip of paper. If old Walt didn't have you in mind when he wrote this, he had hundreds of others like you. He's put into words what I'd like to say to you now—and far better than I could ever express it.

CHARLOTTE:

> What is the quotation? Read it.

DR. JAQUITH:

> No. I'll leave it for you to read. 'Bye.

He gives her the paper and exits. She unfolds the paper and reads.

34A. INSERT TYPED QUOTATION
Untold want, by life and land
      ne'er granted,
Now, Voyager, sail thou forth,
      to seek and find.

    Whitman

DISSOLVE TO:

35. EXT. AN EXPANSE OF BLUE SKY
Across the sky a single gull soars, then another and another until the space is filled with gulls rising, falling, circling. Camera moves downward to

DISSOLVE TO:

36. TOP OF SHIP
The rounded, brightly painted form of a ship's funnel rises into scene. There is no movement of the funnel. The ship is anchored. We see a mast with a pennant hanging on it. There is the sound of whistles and horns of small craft, rather faint, as if coming from the distance. Three deep blasts, also as if coming from the distance. Suddenly there rends the air three deeper blasts, so loud that the vibration is registered on the screen. Camera continues down to

DISSOLVE TO:

37. EXT. PASSENGER LINER
Camera pans down the side of the ship to the waterline. A tender filled with cruise passengers is moored to a gangway. This is the last tender to take off for a shore trip and it is being delayed for a late arrival. The passengers are discussing the reason for the delay, ad lib, with Mr. Thompson, the cruise manager.

PASSENGER:
    The others have all gone. What are we waiting for, Mr. Thompson?

MR. THOMPSON:

For Miss Beauchamp. She said—(He looks up toward the gangway nervously and clears his throat.)

SECOND PASSENGER:

Miss Beauchamp! Why she hasn't stuck her nose out of her cabin since we left New York.

THIRD PASSENGER:

I caught a glimpse of her once—just a glimpse. I think she's been ill. She looks pale and interesting.

A MALE PASSENGER:

She'd be a darn sight more interesting if she wouldn't hold us up.

MR. THOMPSON (warning):

Sssh! (He looks up at the gangway. The others do, too.)

38. THE GANGWAY   MED. SHOT

The woman they have been speaking of walks down into scene, first her feet appearing, then finally her whole person. (NOTE: This should be sharply reminiscent of Charlotte's introduction in the Vale home in Boston.) It is not surprising that at first we do not recognize this woman as Charlotte. A most striking change has taken place in her appearance. She has lost twenty or thirty pounds. Her eyebrows are plucked. She wears no glasses. Her hair is cropped short in a most interesting coiffure, with a widow's peak fore and aft. She is dressed in the conservative good taste that is expensive. We are soon to understand, however, that the transformation is completely an outward one of appearance and not at all an inward one of feeling. She is most uncomfortable in her clothes. She feels like a masquerader. She is self-conscious and is trying hard not to appear as frightened as she feels. Camera pans down with her to the foot of the gangway where Mr. Thompson comes fussily in to help her into the boat.

MR. THOMPSON:
Ah, Miss Beauchamp, here you are. We've been waiting.

CHARLOTTE:
Sorry.

As the tender is cast off, she selects a seat as far re-moved from the other passengers as possible

39.   MED. LONG SHOT   THE TENDER
moves away from the ship.

40.   IN THE TENDER   PAN SHOT   MR. THOMPSON AND JERRY DURRANCE
Mr. Thompson is leading Jerry toward the prow of the boat where Charlotte is sitting. Jerry is a fine-looking, handsome man. He is obviously a cruise passenger and not ashamed of it—photographic paraphernalia is strapped all over him, his coat pockets bulge with guidebooks. Occasionally Mr. Thompson murmurs "Ex-cuse me" or "So sorry" to some of the passengers on whose toes he steps, and all the while he keeps up an ad lib running line to Jerry.

MR. THOMPSON:
Easy does it . . . So sorry . . . We'll make it . . . Uh-uh! caution is the watchword . . . Here we are! (They arrive at Charlotte.) Miss Beauchamp . . . (She doesn't seem to have heard.) Miss Beauchamp . . . (He touches her on the shoulder. She looks up at him, startled and frightened.) Allow me to introduce Mr. Durrance.

A splutter of the tender's engine obliterates the name. Charlotte looks at Jerry uncertainly.

JERRY (cordially):
How do you do!

MR. THOMPSON:
> I've been checking our shore vehicles and there's only one left. Would you be so kind as to share your carriage with this gentleman?

CHARLOTTE:
> Well, really, I—

MR. THOMPSON:
> That's splendid of you, Miss Beauchamp. You're traveling alone and he's traveling alone, and so—(A gesture implies the fitness of the arrangement.) Splendid! (He moves away.)

41.   CLOSE-UP   CHARLOTTE
She is really suffering great pangs of self-consciousness as she looks from one to the other and then looks away.

JERRY'S VOICE:
> I know it's an inconvenience. If it's too much, just say so.

As Charlotte continues to hesitate,
                                            FLASH BACK TO:

42.   DECK OF LINER IN NEW YORK
CLOSE SHOT   CHARLOTTE AND DR. JAQUITH
They are standing at the head of the gangplank. He has hold of her shoulders and is saying his parting words.

DR. JAQUITH:
> Now, pull your own weight! I've taught you the technique. Use it. Forget you're a hidebound New Englander and unbend. Take part! Contribute! Be interested in everything and everybody. Be nice to every human being who crosses your path.
                                            DISSOLVE TO:

43.   TENDER   TWO-SHOT   JERRY AND CHARLOTTE

JERRY:
> You're sure you don't mind?

CHARLOTTE (as warmly as she knows how):
> Of course not. (Then.) I ought to be able to stand it if you can.

He looks at her rather oddly at this remark and doesn't know how to answer, so he doesn't answer anything. With the burden of conversation still on him, he says:

JERRY:
> Are you a typical tourist? I am. Not that you wouldn't know—(With a laugh he indicates the photographic paraphernalia and the guidebooks.) I say it's foolish not to be when you're seeing something you haven't seen before. I hope you want to see everything, the— (Mentions some point of interest.) Why are you smiling?

CHARLOTTE:
> I was thinking of my mother.

JERRY (doesn't understand):
> Oh? Your mother?

43A.   CLOSE-UP   CHARLOTTE
Camera moves to huge close-up of her eyes and forehead as Mrs. Vale's voice comes over.

MRS. VALE'S VOICE:
> Could we try to remember we are hardly commercial travelers? It's bad enough associating with these tourists on board without—

43B.   BACK TO TWO-SHOT
CHARLOTTE (as if in defiant answer):
> I'll be *glad* to see anything you like.

JERRY:
> Thank you. You're a good sport.

>> DISSOLVE TO:

44.   EXT. TERRACE DINING PLACE   OVERLOOKING THE SEA
Here the passengers from the boat are having lunch.

Now, Voyager

Camera pans across the terrace to pick up Jerry and Charlotte's table in foreground. They are finishing dessert. Her eyes are on her plate. Both are silent and occasionally he looks at her as if he is still trying to fathom the mystery behind her. Presently their glance happens to meet. He smiles broadly and she answers timidly.

JERRY:
The baba all right? (He means her baba au rhum.)

CHARLOTTE:
Excellent.

JERRY:
Good. (Then.) Would you excuse me long enough to send a cable? I promised my wife. I should have sent it this morning. Isobel gets nervous.

CHARLOTTE:
Of course you must send it at once.

He rises and offers his cigarette case.

JERRY:
Here, while I'm gone. (She hesitates, and then takes a cigarette. As he lights it for her their eyes meet again.) I wish I understood you.

Charlotte takes the first puff of her cigarette cautiously, almost coughs, but doesn't.

CHARLOTTE:
Since we just met this morning, how could you possibly?

JERRY:
Well, I won't be long.

He exits. Camera moves closer to Charlotte. There is a very strange expression on her face and she murmurs to herself.

90

CHARLOTTE (quietly):
> *He* wishes he understood me.

At this moment she heartily wishes she understood herself, or what she is doing here with this strange man.
She looks at the cigarette she is smoking, quickly lays it
down. She looks at her clothes. She opens her bag and
takes out a mirror and looks at her face, staring at it as
she would a stranger's face. Her hand goes to the back
of her neck where the short cropped widow's peak makes
her neck feel so naked.

CHARLOTTE:
> *He* wishes.

FLASH BACK TO:

45. INT. BOOTH OF BEAUTY SALON
Pan in with Lisa and M. Henri, the proprietor.

LISA:
> Charlotte?

Then she stops short, aghast at the sight of Charlotte in
a chair. A manicurist is working on her nails. Celestine
is plucking her eyebrows. Her head is swathed in a cloth.
She is lying back with her eyes closed.

LISA:
> Celestine! I said nothing about eyebrows. How did
> you ever come to do such a thing?

CELESTINE:
> Because they were terra-ble, madame. She said do
> anything I desire. She did not care.

CHARLOTTE:
> I don't care.

M. HENRI:
> Chitchat, chitchat over eyebrows! What does it mat-
> ter? It is the hair! Regardez!

He removes the towel from Charlotte's head, whips it

off for the effect, revealing Charlotte's spectacular coiffure. Lisa's jaw drops.

LISA:
    Henri!

M. HENRI:
    She is beautiful, n'est-ce pas?

LISA:
    I leave her with you! I *trust* you—

CHARLOTTE:
    It isn't their fault. I said I didn't care.

LISA (with a weak laugh):
    Well, it's done. (To Charlotte.) But have you seen
    yourself? (Gets a hand mirror.)

CHARLOTTE:
    No.

LISA:
    Then you'd better hold onto something for support.

She puts the mirror in front of Charlotte. Charlotte looks,
starts, stares, almost open-mouthed. Then quickly she
looks over her shoulder to see if anyone is standing behind her. No, the reflection must be really her. Once
more she looks at the mirror, only gradually believing
it. Her hand goes to the back of her neck and her
expression is shocked and bewildered and almost hor-
rified. Camera moves to close-up.[4]

                                        DISSOLVE TO:

46.   BACK TO TERRACE
    Camera pulls back from close-up of Charlotte looking in
    mirror as Jerry returns to the table.

    JERRY:
        Well, that's done. (Quickly Charlotte puts the mirror
        in her handbag.) Miss Beauchamp, I've taken the
        liberty of ordering us Cointreaus.

CHARLOTTE:
I'm not Miss Beauchamp!

The remark is just blurted out, unconsciously; it has come out fiercely under the stress of emotions which have been brought on by her reflections.

JERRY:
I beg your pardon?

CHARLOTTE:
Renee Beauchamp is out in Arizona somewhere.

JERRY:
But this morning the cruise manager introduced you—

CHARLOTTE (still blurting):
I know. And the headwaiter and the deck steward, too—they all think I'm Miss Beauchamp. But the purser knows all about it. I took Renee's space at the last moment. She's a friend of my sister-in-law, Lisa. It was all a trick to get me away from my mother.

JERRY:
Well, frankly, I had been wondering. I've seen Renee Beauchamp do her monologues on the stage.

CHARLOTTE (more hectically):
I'd have corrected the mistake then and there, but there was such a crowd. All morning I've looked for a chance to tell you. But I don't know *why* I tell you. I don't know who you are or what you are—or what I'm doing here with a stranger!

JERRY:
I'm awfully sorry. My name is Durrance. Jeremiah Duveaux Durrance, if you must have the whole, silly thing. My father named me after a professor he was fond of. I was J. D. in college—my wife calls me J. Deuveaux—and I'm Jerry to my friends.

A waiter serves the Cointreaus, and their conversation ceases. When the waiter leaves, he raises his glass and in great appeal says:

JERRY:
Stranger.

And after a moment she raises hers and replies with a little smile.

CHARLOTTE:
Stranger.

JERRY:
Did you decide against telling me who you are?

CHARLOTTE (more quietly):
I'm not quite sure who I am.

JERRY:
You mean really?

CHARLOTTE:
If clothes make the man, then at present I'm my sister-in-law, Lisa. If it's shoes— (Shows him hers.) I'm her daughter, June. We both have adequate feet. If it's who I am inside, I— (She stops, then resumes flatly and with self-deprecation.) If I'm ever on the passenger list, I will appear as C. Vale, V-A-L-E. C. Vale, Boston, Massachusetts.

JERRY:
I've heard of Boston. (Smiles.) And the name Vale, like Bunker Hill, rings a familiar bell. Are you one of the Vales of Boston?

CHARLOTTE:
One of the lesser ones.

JERRY:
Well, which one? I don't even know yet whether it's Miss or Missus.

CHARLOTTE:
>   It's Aunt. Most families have one, you know.

JERRY:
>   But Aunt *what?*

CHARLOTTE (announces flatly):
>   My name is Charlotte Vale. *Miss* Charlotte Vale. (Then
>   abruptly.) Please, let's go!

She hurries out. He sits stunned for a moment. Then,
collecting himself, he quickly gets up, leaves some money
on the table for the waiter, hurries after her.

47.   TERRACE STEPS
as he catches her forcibly by the arm.

JERRY:
>   I was very clumsy. I hope I didn't offend you beyond
>   forgiveness.

CHARLOTTE:
>   I wasn't offended. I think it's funny, too.

JERRY:
>   It's like me to blunder just when I was going to ask
>   you for a favor this afternoon. I have some shopping
>   to do for my daughters and I need a woman's help.
>   I would regard it as a mark of your forgiveness.

CHARLOTTE:
>   Of course. A spinster aunt is just the person to se-
>   lect presents for young girls.

>   DISSOLVE TO:

48.   EXT. SHIP'S TENDER   (PROCESS)   DUSK
CLOSE SHOT   CHARLOTTE AND JERRY IN BOW
There is almost an air of comradeship between them now.
Jerry picks up one of the packages and tosses it up and
down.

JERRY:
> I think we did darn well. The jewelry is just right for Beatrice. At sixteen they get the urge for glamour. And the sweater for Tina . . .

CHARLOTTE:
> How old is Tina?

JERRY:
> Well here—I'll show you.

From a billfold he takes a Kodak snapshot and shows it to her.

JERRY:
> My harem.

49.   INSERT   SNAPSHOT
Standing against a high privet hedge is a girl of sixteen who looks as if she has just come from under a dryer at the hairdresser. She is standing beside a woman who is sitting on a folding wooden settee, knitting. Surely this can't be Jerry's wife! More likely his mother! She is a small woman, flat chested, narrow shouldered, narrow faced. She wears her hair drawn straight back, her head is bent, her eyes are upon her knitting, her lips tightly compressed. Before them, seated cross-legged on the grass, is a girl of seven. She wears glasses and she scowls straight into the camera.

50.   CLOSE SHOT   CHARLOTTE AND JERRY
as she studies the snapshot and he waits for her reaction. You can tell that Charlotte carefully chooses her words when she begins.

CHARLOTTE:
> Who is that knitting?

JERRY:
> That's Isobel, my wife. The picture isn't very good of Isobel. If she had only looked up and smiled!

(Then, somewhat embarrassed, adds.) That's Beatrice by her.

CHARLOTTE:

Then it must be Tina sitting on the grass with her legs crossed.

JERRY:

We hope she won't have to wear glasses always. Tina wouldn't smile for me, either. She's convinced she's an ugly duckling.

CHARLOTTE:

Does Tina know she wasn't wanted?

JERRY (looks sharply at her):

There's an odd remark—

CHARLOTTE:

I don't know why I made it.

JERRY:

I mean odd because it hits so close to the truth. Even before she was born, her mother said—but never mind that. (Then he breaks the mood and speaks in a lighter tone. From his coat pocket he produces a small package. It is wrapped in gay paper and tied with a loop so one can carry it dangling on one's finger. He holds it up before her by the loop.) I hope you'll accept a slight offering for being my guide today. I don't know the first thing about perfumery, but the clerk said this was all right. It's a mixture of several kinds of flowers. It's called Jolies Fleurs. I thought that would be safe as I don't know your preference in flowers.

He drops the little package in her lap. She is glad it is dusk, for she can feel the color mounting to her cheeks. Ridiculous! But she can't remember that any man has ever gone into a shop and bought a present for her. She lifts the little package.

CHARLOTTE:
Thank you so much.

is all she can manage to say at first. The launch arrives
(play it by off-scene sound). Jerry helps her to her feet.
Then she adds,

CHARLOTTE:
I'll put some on my handkerchief tonight.

JERRY:
Will you? Good! And let's meet for a cocktail in the
bar at a quarter of eight.

DISSOLVE TO:

51.   INT. CHARLOTTE'S STATEROOM   (NIGHT)
CHARLOTTE
fresh from the tub, dressed in slip and mules, yanks
open her clothes closet door. She is trying to select
something to wear. The familiar red dinner gown of Lisa's
is good as anything. She pulls it out. Lisa has pinned a
small paper on the shoulder of the dress. Charlotte reads
it, tosses it aside. She begins to put on the dress.

PAN DOWN TO:

52.   INSERT   NOTE FROM DRESS
lying on floor.
    Silver slippers and silver evening bag will be
    found in accessory drawer.

53.   CHARLOTTE
is zipping the dress. It is the shade of a scarlet tanager,
very low, with a square-cut neck in front.

CHARLOTTE (mutters):
I suppose she thought I'd wear oxfords and carry
my shopping bag.

(The following action should be played very quickly.)
    From the accessory drawer she takes the silver slip-
pers and steps into them. She produces the silver bag,

selects a handkerchief, and gives it a shake. She is about to shove it into her bag when she remembers the perfumery. She unseals the stopper of the bottle and draws out the tiny crystal stiletto. She wipes it off on her handkerchief, refuels it twice, and thrusts it, wet and icicle cold, behind each ear.

Then again she searches the closet, this time for something in the way of an evening wrap. At the back of the closet she catches a glimpse of something else scarlet. It proves to be a long cape wrapped around its hanger, lining side out. Unfolding it, she discovers a garment of velvet, the tawny yellow of French mustard, with a conventional design painted on it in various shades of brown, with shimmering silver spots here and there. She throws it quickly around her shoulders. It reaches to below her knees. She doesn't notice the note pinned on it.

She glances into the mirror for one last quick inspection, then stops to gaze longer. Anyone would stop to look twice at what she sees. Not bad, not bad at all. But this stranger in the mirror lacks something. Her lips should be as scarlet as the gown. From the top drawer of the dresser she takes out a box from the beauty parlor labeled Cosmetics. She discovers a small nickel cylinder and applies the lipstick to her lips quickly and skillfully. No secrecy now!

It's not until she gives that last glance around the room that she catches sight of a blue envelope on the round table in the middle of the room. She tears it open.

54.   OUT

55.   OUT

56.   INSERT   RADIOGRAM
        JUST REMEMBER DOWN WITH THAT NEW
        ENGLAND CONSCIENCE   STOP   PLAY THE
        GAME.

                                                    JAQUITH[5]

57.   CHARLOTTE
pushes the radiogram into her evening bag, snaps it shut
with a click, snaps off the electric lights with another
click, and leaves the room, her silver slippers scuttling
along the corridor with the haste of a Cinderella's. She
is already ten minutes late.

WIPE OFF TO:

58.   INT. BAR   AT A TABLE BEFORE AN ARTIFICIAL FIREPLACE
JERRY
is looking at his watch. Then he looks off-scene and his
expression lights up.

59.   FROM HIS PERSPECTIVE   CHARLOTTE
comes to the entrance.

60.   CLOSER ANGLE   CHARLOTTE
stops on the threshold, searching the crowded, smoke-
filled room, not sure that she will recognize him among
so many, not sure he will recognize her. Then she sees
him coming and, camera panning, goes forward. As he
meets her with a smile:

CHARLOTTE:
    I'm late, I know.

JERRY:
    I hoped you hadn't changed your mind. (He leads
    her back to the table and they sit down.)

61.   AT TABLE
A waiter hovers.

JERRY:
    What will you have?

CHARLOTTE (hesitates):
    I'll leave it to you.

JERRY:
    Well, how are bourbon old-fashioneds? (He nods to
    the waiter, who exits.) Will you have a cigarette?

She takes a cigarette and gives a slight cough when he lights it this time. The waiter brings their drinks. When Charlotte looks at Jerry she sees that he is sniffing the air, trying to locate something.

JERRY:
I can smell something sweet. I wonder what it is?

CHARLOTTE (flatly):
It's called Jolies Fleurs.

JERRY:
Oh? (Smiles.) How awfully nice of you.

CHARLOTTE:
I've probably put on too much.

JERRY:
Not for my taste. (He studies her.) I can't seem to pigeonhole you—the way you advance and then re-treat suddenly.

CHARLOTTE:
Then please don't try.

JERRY (again amiably):
All right— You made a striking impression over there as you stood in the doorway looking for me.

CHARLOTTE:
I've probably put on too much lipstick, too.

JERRY:
Not that I notice. I did notice the wrap at once. I don't pretend to know much, but I recognize the fritillaries when I see one.

CHARLOTTE:
I've no idea what you're talking about.

JERRY:
Why, the butterfly design painted on your coat. Do you mind leaning forward? Those long, dark, slen-

der lines coming over your shoulder are supposed
to be your antennae, I think. (Rises and bends over
her.) Hello! What's this?

CHARLOTTE:
What's what?

JERRY:
Something on your cape. Why, it's pinned on! Somebody has been playing a joke on you, I guess.

CHARLOTTE (mortified):
Unpin it, please.

He does so, fumbling so long with the small pin that he
can't help reading whatever Lisa has written.

JERRY:
Here it is. (He passes the paper to her and she reads
it.)

62.   INSERT   NOTE
in Charlotte's hands.
I had no evening coat that was right, so Renee
wants to contribute hers. She says it always
makes an impression, and has always given her
a good time. She hopes it will do the same for
you.

63.   BACK TO SCENE
as Charlotte gives a short, derogatory laugh and passes
the paper back to him.

CHARLOTTE:
Well, this ought to pigeonhole me for you, all right.

JERRY (studies the note):
What does it mean? I can't make head or tail of it.

CHARLOTTE:
Why, this cape belongs to your friend, Renee Beauchamp. She lent it to me.

JERRY:

> Oh, I say! (He exclaims with delight.) Your wings are borrowed! Well, they suit you, just the same.

CHARLOTTE:

> No, they don't! They don't suit me in the least![6] (She takes the paper, tears it into small bits, and shoves them into her bag.) You were quite right when you said someone was playing a joke on me. (She rises, slipping the cape off her shoulders and throwing it over her arm.)

JERRY (rising, too):

> You aren't going, are you? Please don't yet.

Suddenly, from off scene, a voice calls out.

MACK'S VOICE:

> J. D.!

Jerry looks off and registers surprise and pleasure.

64. WIDER ANGLE

to include Frank McIntyre and his wife, Deb, old friends of Jerry's. An enthusiastic greeting.

JERRY:

> Mack! And Deb, too! Well, as I'm alive!

DEB:

> Hi!

MACK:

> We saw your name on the passenger list. What are you doing down here?

JERRY:

> Business. I'm going to Rio.

Business of shaking hands, and Deb kisses Jerry.

DEB:

> We've been here for weeks. We're joining the cruise!

JERRY (to Charlotte):
These are my old friends, Deb McIntyre and Frank. And my new friend, Miss—(Hesitates only the fraction of a second.) Beauchamp.

CHARLOTTE (is afraid of meeting people):
How do you do?

Deb is giving her a sharp appraisal. For the first time in Charlotte's life, another woman finds her passing muster.

DEB (puts out her hand warmly):
How do you do?

MACK:
Don't tell me this is the famous Beauchamp, the one who does the imitations?

JERRY:
Oh. Another one altogether. This is—Camille Beauchamp.

MACK:
Well, come up to the club. We've got a table. We can have dinner and we can have a dance.

DEB (to Charlotte):
Won't you join us, Miss Beauchamp?

CHARLOTTE:
Thank you, I don't dance.

JERRY:
Good. That lets me out, too. I don't dance either, according to my daughters.

DEB:
How are Isobel and the kids?

JERRY:
Fine when I left.

MACK:
> Give our best when you write.

During last three speeches Charlotte murmurs "Good night" and slips away. As suddenly Jerry notices that she is gone,

WIPE OFF TO:

65.   EXT. DECK   TRUCKING SHOT
Charlotte is walking rapidly away. Jerry chases after her and catches her at rail.

JERRY:
> Wait a minute! Why did you run out on me like that?

CHARLOTTE:
> I was tired . . . I'll have dinner in my cabin . . . and you'll want to be with your friends . . .

JERRY:
> There's something more.

CHARLOTTE:
> Why did you introduce me in that way?

JERRY:
> It wasn't up to me to let the cat out of the bag. Did I do wrong?

CHARLOTTE:
> Well, it doesn't make my situation on this cruise any easier.

JERRY:
> Then why didn't you stop me?

CHARLOTTE:
> I hadn't the courage. I haven't any backbone.[7] And then, when you came out with that "Camille"—

JERRY:
> Well, it was the only French name I could think of except Fifi.

CHARLOTTE.:
> I suppose that is meant to be funny. (She turns away from him to the rail.)

JERRY:
> My wife calls my lighter moments "trying to be funny." But I intended it as a compliment. In that dress you're rather like a camellia.

CHARLOTTE:
> Likely! (She turns her face further away and a sharp look of pain crosses it.)

JERRY:
> I don't quite know how I've offended you. I don't understand you at all.

CHARLOTTE (bitterly):
> Perhaps this will help you. You showed me your album—I should show you mine. Here! A picture of my family.

From her bag she produces a small photograph. She pushes it at him. He takes it, looks at it, and, after a moment, whistles.

JERRY:
> Family is right. (He points to one of the figures in the photograph.)

65A.   INSERT   PHOTOGRAPH
of Charlotte, her mother, her brothers and their wives, and Lisa and June. It is a group picture which has been taken in the Boston home during some family festivity. Jerry's finger is pointing at Mrs. Vale.

JERRY'S VOICE:
> Your grandmother?

CHARLOTTE'S VOICE:
> No. My mother.

65B.   BACK TO SCENE

JERRY:
    A very strong character, I'd say. And these?

CHARLOTTE:
    My brothers and their wives.

JERRY:
    But they're so much older. Oh, I see—the adored
    little sister.

CHARLOTTE:
    Scarcely. And there's Lisa and her daughter, June . . .

JERRY:
    And who is the fat lady with the heavy brows and
    all the hair?

CHARLOTTE:
    That's a poor, pathetic spinster aunt.

JERRY:
    Where are *you?* Taking the picture?

CHARLOTTE (after just a moment's hesitation lets it tear
out):
    I'm the fat lady with the heavy brows and all the
    hair. I'm poor Aunt Charlotte. And I have been ill. I
    have been in a sanitarium the last three months. And
    I'm not well yet. And—

Breaking, she makes a move to run away. Her hand is
on the rail. He quickly covers it with his, detaining her.
She stops but she doesn't look back at him. He leaves
his hand on hers and there is a silent communion of
sympathy. After a long time:

JERRY:
    Forgive me. (She looks at him and smiles warmly.)
    Feeling better?

CHARLOTTE:
> Much. Thanks to you. Oh, many thanks to you.

JERRY:
> For what?

CHARLOTTE (lightly):
> For sharing the carriage. For walking my legs off sightseeing. For lunch, for shopping. (And then soberly.) And for helping me have a few moments when I felt almost alive. Thank you.

JERRY:
> Thank you, who?

CHARLOTTE:
> Thank you, Jerry.

JERRY:
> I had a wonderful day. Can we have another tomorrow? Will you meet me at nine thirty for breakfast?

CHARLOTTE:
> I think so.

JERRY:
> Sleep well, Camille. (Offers his hand.)

CHARLOTTE (takes it):
> Good night.

Then, as she walks swiftly away,

DISSOLVE TO:

66.   INT. CHARLOTTE'S CABIN
Charlotte comes in. Her spirit is light and airy. In placing her bag on the dressing table she catches sight of herself in the mirror. Once more she studies the woman reflected there, the woman in the red dress whom Jerry has compared with a camellia. She looks with confidence and with happiness. But then, as she looks further, her expression becomes sober.

67.   ANGLE PAST CHARLOTTE IN THE MIRROR
Charlotte and the woman in the glass seem to be study-
ing each other, and the longer Charlotte studies, the more
she realizes that the reflected woman is just a sham and
not true at all. In fact, now the reflection in the mirror
changes to that of "Aunt Charlotte," ugly and fat, with
beetle brows that meet in the middle, and too much hair.

68.   CLOSE-UP   CHARLOTTE
The most acute pain of disillusion strikes her. A sound
that is first a derisive laugh of self-contempt, then changes
almost into a sob, comes out of her.
                                             DISSOLVE TO:

69.   INT. JERRY'S CABIN   JERRY
is at the dressing table writing a letter.

70.   INSERT OF LETTER
as he writes.
          Dear Tina:
          I was sorry to see you in tears when I left, but
          Daddy understood— You were crying because
          you were being left alone. But today I made a
          discovery—all people are alone in some ways
          and some people are alone in all ways. Even after
          someone is grown up she can be alone—

71.   JERRY
continues writing. Suddenly he stops as he hears the
engines of the ship starting. He listens.
                                             DISSOLVE TO:

72.   STERN OF SHIP AT WATERLINE
The propellers stir up the water. We hear the sound.
                                             DISSOLVE TO:

73.   INT. CHARLOTTE'S CABIN   TRUCKING SHOT
moving across the room to her where she is sleeping.
Keep in the sound of the propellers. As we reach a close-

up of her, this sound gradually sharpens into a peculiar whine—a sustained note of music—and gradually we
DISSOLVE TO:

74.   WHAT CHARLOTTE DREAMS
She is a young girl again, on that trip with her mother. She is seated in the ballroom of the ship, at the edge of the dance floor, and the music we hear is an old-fashioned waltz. She wears her glasses. There is a wistful look on her face, and we realize no one ever asks her to dance.

But then a young officer approaches her, Leslie again, and stops in front of her and says:

LESLIE:
May I have this dance?

Quickly Charlotte looks over her shoulder, thinking he must be speaking to someone beyond her, but when she looks back, he again says:

LESLIE:
May I have this dance, please?

CHARLOTTE (flustered):
I don't dance.

LESLIE:
Would you like to walk on deck, then?

CHARLOTTE:
Me?

LESLIE:
You and I, yes. I've been watching you. Will you?

It is almost too much for Charlotte to believe. In her embarrassment she takes off her glasses and looks away, and then looks back at him. He looks steadily at her. Tremblingly, she rises to her feet. She nods and moves away and he follows.

Now the scene dissolves to the upper deck, to Charlotte and Leslie seated together in the moonlight. His arm is around her. He gathers her in and they kiss.

Suddenly there is a peculiar cut-away to the figure of Mrs. Vale, Charlotte's mother. Zoom her figure right up into close-up. She stares, outraged.

MRS. VALE:
Charlotte, whom are you kissing?

Cut to Charlotte. She looks first in the direction of her mother, and then at Leslie. Suddenly her face is suffused with the utmost shock. We cut to the man she has been kissing. It is not Leslie at all. It is Jerry.

DISSOLVE TO:

75.   CABIN   CLOSE-UP   CHARLOTTE
suddenly awake with a gasp, sits up in bed. The effect should be that of her sitting upright out of her dream, which is suddenly cut off, and we are back, on her gasp, to actuality. Charlotte is trembling violently; the emotional impact of having dreamed of kissing Jerry is terrific. She looks wildly about, then looks out of the porthole. Camera moves up to the porthole. The moon is shining brightly and the ship is peacefully in motion.

DISSOLVE TO:

76.   PORTHOLE IN JERRY'S CABIN
Pull back to him. Propped up in bed with his reading light on he, too, is looking out of the porthole—reflectively, soberly. He has not been able to sleep and that is why he has been reading. His eyes return to the book he is reading. Something on the page catches his eye and he reaches for a pencil.

77.   INSERT   A PAGE OF WALT WHITMAN'S POETRY
Jerry's hand enters scene and the pencil marks the part that has caught his eye. Camera moves up and centers on it and we read:

Untold want, by life and land ne'er
    granted,

Now, Voyager, sail thou forth, to
  seek and find.

Then the background of the insert changes to a super-
imposed shot of the wake of the ship. It is as if the words
were suspended in the water that is being churned up
as the ship sails on.[8]

FADE OUT

FADE IN
78. INSERT
  devised to show the progress of the cruise ship down
  through the Caribbean and along the coast of Brazil to
  the mouth of the harbor of Rio de Janeiro.

DISSOLVE TO:

79. EXT. SPORTS DECK JERRY AND MACK
  are having a set of deck tennis. They whoop it up like
  boys. After a particularly fast set-to, which Jerry wins,
  he looks up at the upper half deck and, laughing, raises
  his own hands in sign of victory. Pan camera up to the
  upper half deck to Charlotte and Deb, seated by the railing. The girls wave back.

80. UPPER DECK CHARLOTTE AND DEB
  are stretched out in deck chairs, sunning themselves in
  the luxurious tropical sun. Their bodies glisten with oil,
  which they occasionally replenish. They wear abbrevi-
  ated tropical clothes.

DEB:
  I haven't heard Jerry laugh like that in years.

CHARLOTTE:
  Really?

DEB:
  You're good for him.

CHARLOTTE:
  He's good to me!

DEB:

> Well, have a good time. I expect you both deserve the break. Charlotte dear, you've been frank with me. May I be frank with you?

CHARLOTTE:

> About what?

DEB:

> Charlotte dear, how much do you know about his life at home?

CHARLOTTE:

> I know he's married. He showed me a snapshot of his family. He seemed very proud of them, too.

DEB:

> He would. Right out of the age of chivalry, that boy. Well, I can tell you there's not much joy in life for him at home.

CHARLOTTE:

> If there was anything Jerry wanted me to know, I think he'd have told me, himself.

DEB:

> *I* want you to know and *I'm* telling you. Honestly, when I see what a woman like Isobel can do to a man like Jerry, it makes me boil.

CHARLOTTE:

> No man has to stand it.

DEB:

> The weak have great strength, you know, when they're clinging to something decent and fine. He's been cursed from the first day he met Isobel by a ruling passion not to hurt her.

CHARLOTTE:

> It must have been more. He married her.

DEB:

Propinquity, my dear. *And* propriety. Isobel was one of those pure, high-minded girls who believed that a kiss required a proposal of marriage . . . and she's been about his neck ever since. Well, he struggled at his architecture to get together enough money.

CHARLOTTE:

Architecture? He told me he was some kind of electrical jobber.

DEB:

Now he is.

CHARLOTTE:

But why did he give it up?

DEB:

Because Isobel kept reminding him he was now a married man with financial responsibilities. Then, almost immediately, she found she was going to have a child. She considered herself a great martyr and she's played the martyr ever since. That's her grasp on him, her martyrdom—and her jealousy.

CHARLOTTE:

Has she any reason to be jealous?

DEB:

If you mean does Jerry have flings with other women, no. But mostly she's jealous of Tina.

CHARLOTTE:

Jealous of a child?

DEB:

Yes—of the child she never wanted. Do you know that before Tina was born Isobel actually went to a doctor and tried to get him to say that her health wouldn't permit her to have a child? And yet, if you could hear her sanctimonious maternal tone when she lets it leak out what a self-sacrificing mother she's been! Gosh!

CHARLOTTE:
Really, Deb—I won't listen.

MACK'S VOICE (off-scene):
Hey!

81. WIDER ANGLE
to include Jerry and Mack as they enter, puffing from their exercise, interrupting the scene.

CHARLOTTE:
Who won?

MACK (to Jerry):
Don't brag.

JERRY (to the girls):
What are you two so thick about?

DEB (guiltily):
We were just being girls together.

JERRY:
Oh?

He looks closely from her to Charlotte. Charlotte evades his look, looks off.

CHARLOTTE:
Look, we're getting into harbor!

She gets up and exits to the rail. Jerry, with his look fixed firmly on her, follows. Mack would follow, too, but Deb pulls him by his sleeve and gives him a significant look. He looks at her, surprised, and then gets it.

82. RAILING   CHARLOTTE
is looking off as Jerry comes in. She feels his presence as he comes to the rail beside her, looking directly at her.

CHARLOTTE:

> Look, Jerry. It's the one sight in the world that's better than the picture postcards.

JERRY:

> What was Deb saying?

CHARLOTTE:

> Oh, you know Deb. She was rattling on . . .

JERRY:

> About me? I don't mind if she was, but I'd like to know.

CHARLOTTE:

> Yes. (Looks at him.) She was telling me about your life at home.

JERRY:

> Oh.

A sharp shadow of pain goes across his face. He turns away. His hand is on the rail. She covers it with hers and there is a silent communion of sympathy. This time, in contrast to a previous time, the sympathy flows from her to him.

CHARLOTTE:

> You shouldn't miss this moment, Jerry. There's only one first sailing into Rio Harbor. See, over there

JERRY (still looking away):

> This is my getting-off place. Your boat goes on in three days. Will I see you?

CHARLOTTE:

> Not unless you pay more attention to your guide.

He looks at her and then smiles.

JERRY:

> Thank you.

CHARLOTTE:
On your left—over there—

He looks at her for a moment longer and then looks off in the direction she is indicating.

JERRY:
Sugar Loaf?

CHARLOTTE (warmly and gaily):
We'll take the cable car to the top. And that stretch of sand—Copacabana Beach—we can get brown as Indians in three days.

JERRY:
Copacabana. There's music in the word.

CHARLOTTE:
And up on that mountain there's something to please your architect's heart—

JERRY (looks sharply at her):
Did Deb tell you I used to be an architect?

CHARLOTTE:
Look at it, Jerry the Christus statue. You wouldn't think from here that there's a way to get to the top. But we will. They say it's the closest you can get to heaven.

DISSOLVE TO:

83. A SERIES OF ATMOSPHERIC SHOTS OF RIO DE JANEIRO
This series should be of considerable length, not only to tell the character and charm of this wonderful city, but to get over a time lapse of more than one day. For this latter reason, both day and night shots should be used. Music, of course, with this. This series finishes with

DISSOLVE TO:

84. STOCK SHOT OF RIO
angling down from the heights of a road.

85. LONG SHOT   THE ROAD
A ramshackle car is moving up the grade.

86. OUT

87. INT. THE CAR
It is being driven by Manoel, a swarthy-skinned Portuguese. In the back seat are Charlotte and Jerry. The car
is sputtering and coughing, and its progress is very slow.

JERRY (is fussing about it):
Serves me right for picking up a car because I liked
the face of the driver instead of getting one from a
regular tourist agency.

CHARLOTTE (good-naturedly):
Well, don't fuss. It doesn't matter.

JERRY:
But we promised to meet Deb and Mack up there
for dinner.

CHARLOTTE:
How much further is it?

JERRY (calls to the driver):
Manoel! Manoel!

MANOEL (turns around and grins):
Okay, senhor.

JERRY:
Don't look, just listen. How far is it?

MANOEL:
Banana trees.

JERRY:
No, no! Distance. Miles. Kilometers. Combien? Dis-
tance-si-ong—

(NOTE: Any Italian words or dialect above, or that follow,
should be translated into Portuguese.)

MANOEL:
Bananas, sapodillos, papayas, monkeys, parrots, rubber.

JERRY:
And the sign on his windshield said "English-spoking driver."

CHARLOTTE:
What he needs is a couple of good Portuguese-spoking passengers. Now just settle back and— (Stops in sudden fright.)

88.   MED. SHOT   THE CAR
abruptly drives off the road onto a small, unpaved side road.

89.   THE CAR   CHARLOTTE AND JERRY

CHARLOTTE (just catching her breath):
Now where is he going?

JERRY:
This must be the shortcut I told you about, past the old church I wanted to see.

DISSOLVE TO:

90.   THE SIDE ROAD NEAR TOP OF MOUNTAIN
The car emerges from a thick white cloud into view. In fact, they are above a layer of clouds now which completely obscures the country below. The road is much narrower now and much rougher. The car jounces along.

91.   INT. CAR   CHARLOTTE AND JERRY
are bouncing in the back seat.

CHARLOTTE:
Are you sure this is the right way?

JERRY:
I'll bet he doesn't have any more idea where he is than we do. I'll make him turn around.

CHARLOTTE:
>It's no use. You'll only get "Okay, senhor, banana trees."

92.   WIDER ANGLE   TO INCLUDE MANOEL
as Jerry leans forward and taps him on the shoulder.

JERRY:
>Manoel! Turn the car around.

MANOEL:
>Okay, senhor. (Drives cheerfully on.)

CHARLOTTE:
>I told you.

JERRY (louder):
>Manoel! Stop! *Turn around!* GO BACK! (He accompanies this with very large gestures.)

MANOEL (bewildered; in Portuguese):
>I am to turn around and go back?

JERRY:
>I think so. Try it, anyway.

MANOEL:
>Si, si. Oui, oui. Okay, senhor.

93.   MED. SHOT   THE CAR
as Manoel abruptly turns it in to the mountain side of the road, stops it with a jolt, then starts to back. The road is very narrow here, and on the other side drops away, but the bushes and fog obscure what it drops away into. Manoel backs the car quite rapidly almost to the edge until we hear:

JERRY'S VOICE (from inside car):
>Stop!

And Manoel stops the car with a jolt.

94.   INT. CAR   GROUP

JERRY:
   Take it easy, man. Go forward.

MANOEL (agreeably):
   Si, si. Forward. (And he, too, points. He shifts gears.)

95.   INSERT   GEAR SHIFT
The gear shift catches. Manoel shifts it several times, finally winding up right back in reverse.

96.   GROUP   IN CAR

MANOEL (proudly):
   Forward. (He jams on the gas.)

97.   MED. SHOT   CAR
It backs right off the road and disappears. A split second later there is a crash.

98.   LEDGE   BELOW ROAD
The car has dropped onto a wide ledge that is just a few feet below the surface of the road. The car has turned over and the wheels are spinning. There is absolute silence for a moment, then we hear Manoel's piercing screams of fright. (This shot should establish that nearby there is a little crumbling shed or shelter made from banana tree branches.)

99.   FRONT WINDOW OF CAR
Manoel crawls out. He is hysterical. A stream of Portuguese comes out of him like a river.

MANOEL (in Portuguese):
   Mother in heaven, what have I done? I said go forward, the car went backward. Are you killed? Are you hurt? (Runs to back window.) Dear senhor and senhora, are your dead? (He raps on the window. The window is being rolled down. Now Manoel

watches it in an agony of suspense, just muttering
to himself. Through the window appears first Jerry's
head and then Charlotte's. At the sight of them
Manoel falls down on his knees and with his hands
clasped to his bosom continues.) Please, senhor and
senhora, don't be hurt. Please, don't be killed.

Jerry and Charlotte look around, at first a little bewildered. Then they look at each other and start to laugh.
At this Manoel breaks into sobs of joy.

100.   ANOTHER ANGLE
Jerry crawls out and then pulls Charlotte out. In the
meantime Manoel gets to his feet. At the sight of the car
and the realization of what a wreck it is, his sobs turn
to sobs of grief.

MANOEL (in Portuguese):
     Oh, the car. The formerly so beautiful car! (He leans
     against one of the tires and the tears pour forth.)

JERRY:
     Sure you're not hurt?

CHARLOTTE:
     Not a scratch.

JERRY:
     Then suppose you try to control our hysterical friend
     while I try to fish out our stuff.

As Jerry crawls partway under again and brings out their
topcoats and a small suitcase of Charlotte's, she goes to
the front of the car to Manoel.

CHARLOTTE:
     Don't cry Manoel. It's all right. (lays her hand on his
     shoulder.)

At the touch of her hand, Manoel looks up with the
tears streaming down his face. Then he makes a gesture
toward the car and once more buries his head in sobs.

CHARLOTTE (to Jerry):
I'm afraid he's inconsolable.

JERRY:
I'll try.

As he comes to Manoel, the latter cowers back in fear, sure he is going to be punished. He again breaks into a torrent of Portuguese.

MANOEL (in Portuguese):
I tell her to go forward and she go backward. Please, senhor, I will descend into the valley to get cavallo-e-corda while senhor and senhora remain in the car. Cavallo-e-corda, cavallo-e-corda—(He repeats again and again as he runs away.)

JERRY:
What did he say?

CHARLOTTE:
I hope he said he'll get a horse and rope.

DISSOLVE TO:

101–104. OMITTED

105. AT THE CAR — DUSK RAIN

A violent tropical storm is beating down on the car. There is a considerable wind, too. Camera pans over to the shelter.

DISSOLVE TO:

106. OMITTED

107. INT. SHELTER — NIGHT

The rain has stopped, but heavy drops still trickle from the trees and the roof of the shelter. A fire blazes. Seated behind it, wearing their topcoats, Charlotte and Jerry are finishing a dinner of bread, fruit, and coffee, using her suitcase for a table.

JERRY:

> At least we can thank Manoel for leaving us his lunch box.

CHARLOTTE:

> And you make a very satisfactory Robinson Crusoe.

JERRY:

> Well, Tina and I do a little roughing it once in a while! Tina loves the woods, and is a great child in such a setting.

CHARLOTTE:

> You seem to be very close to Tina.

JERRY:

> I've tried to be. I've always felt responsible for Tina's existence, which she never asked for, and which she has found so full of difficulties, poor kid.

CHARLOTTE:

> Yes, I think I can understand Tina. She reminds me a little of myself.

JERRY:

> Say, you're cold. Your teeth are chattering. Turn around. I'm going to pound your back till you yell for mercy.

CHARLOTTE:

> Yes, sir. (She turns around. He pounds her back.)

JERRY:

> You know you're going to miss your boat.

CHARLOTTE:

> Well, I've no one on board who will lie awake worrying.

JERRY:

> You're a good sport.

CHARLOTTE:

Nonsense! This is the first thrilling experience I've ever had in my life!

JERRY (soberly):

You'd better tell me all Deb said to you.

CHARLOTTE:

Why did you give up architecture, Jerry? How could you? Why, when I see the light that comes into your eyes just when you look at a beautiful building . . .

JERRY:

Architecture gave me up. The Depression came along. I started my little business on borrowed money. Gradually I slipped into a hole I can't climb out of. A prolonged sense of failure can do things that can't be corrected. You ought to know. You're one to talk.

CHARLOTTE:

Yes, I'm one to talk. Look what a prolonged sense of failure did to me.

He turns her around and feels her hands.

JERRY:

You're still cold. Here, I've got a bottle of reviver I've been saving. (He takes a bottle of whiskey from his pocket, pours some in the top of Manuel's thermos bottle, hands it to her.) Drink up.

CHARLOTTE:

All of it?

JERRY:

You won't know what hit you.

He gets up and puts some wood on the fire. She drinks some whiskey with a shudder, pours the remainder of the bottle into the top of the thermos jug.

CHARLOTTE:
> Your turn.

He drinks it off, also with a shudder.

JERRY:
> You know, we're either going to have to bundle or freeze tonight. Two light topcoats and one blanket.

CHARLOTTE:
> Well—they tell me bundling is a New England custom that is reverenced and honored.

DISSOLVE TO:

108.   THE SKY
The middle of the night. Moonlight shining on the jungle. The storm clouds passing. A most beautiful sight.

DISSOLVE TO:

109.   TRUCKING SHOT   APPROACHING THE SHELTER
First pick up the fire, dying embers. Then move on to Jerry and Charlotte. Asleep. She lies at an angle from him but her head is on his chest. Move up very close. Charlotte wakens. At first there is a little start until she realizes where she is. Then she looks at him, sees that he is sound asleep, as relaxed and rumpled as a small boy. She looks down at his chest, slowly realizing that she has been using it as a pillow. She hears something and bends her ear close. It is the steady thumping of his heart she hears. We hear it, too. Bring up the sound. Odd to hear the sound of a man's heart. Odd and wonderful. She lays her head down onto his chest again and goes to sleep.

DISSOLVE TO:

110.   THE SKY AGAIN
Later in the night. The moon is setting now. Bring up music, some theme which we have always used to express the hopelessness of the romantic side of Charlotte's nature—a weird, dreamlike rendition of this music.

DISSOLVE TO:

111.   OMITTED

        FADE IN
112.   THE SKY AGAIN   DAWN
        The sun is coming up through the clouds.

                                            DISSOLVE TO:

113–118. EXT. THE SHELTER
        A little way away Jerry is seated on a ledge, smoking a
        cigarette. After a moment he hears a sound from the
        shelter and looks toward it. Charlotte appears from in-
        side the shelter. She stops as she sees him.

        JERRY:
            Good morning.

        CHARLOTTE:
            Good morning. (Her voice is a little unsteady.) Why
            didn't you wake me?

        JERRY:
            Oh—you looked too comfortable. (He gets up, goes
            over to her. Camera goes with him.) You look very
            pretty in the morning light, Camille. How do you
            feel?

        CHARLOTTE:
            Fine. (A slight pause.) I had a good night's sleep.

        JERRY:
            No dream?

        CHARLOTTE:
            Yes. A dream.

        JERRY:
            I had a dream. When I woke up this morning, I found
            it was a reality.

        CHARLOTTE (looks away):
            I don't know what you can think of me. It was be-
            cause of that strong drink. I'm not accustomed to it.

                            127

JERRY:
>   Well, I have no such excuse to offer, so what can you think of me? Married. Tied hand and foot to a situation I've got to go back to.

CHARLOTTE:
>   Well, don't let it worry you. I've got a situation I've got to go back to, also. I don't see that any harm has been done to your situation or to mine, either. A kiss. Over now. Soon forgotten. In fact—(Her tone has become mocking.) in case your conscience may be troubling you, you've probably done me a good turn. Dr. Jaquith once suggested that a flirtation would be excellent for me. It's a very effective measure for pulling one out of a depression. (She gives him a twisted, sarcastic smile.)

JERRY (shortly):
>   Don't, please. (A rather long, silent pause.) We'll have to hike it, I guess, to the nearest settlement.[9]

119.   OMITTED

120.   INT. A WAYSIDE RESTAURANT
Charlotte is seated at a table, toying with a cup of coffee. In background Jerry is at a wall telephone, just ending a conversation with a goodbye. Dishes on the table let us know they have just finished breakfast.

JERRY:
>   The tourist company is sending a car. The boat waited last night for two hours. I had them wire to Mack and Deb that we're safe. You can rejoin the cruise at Buenos Aires.

CHARLOTTE:
>   How can I?

JERRY:
>   Fly. There's a plane going down first thing in the morning.

CHARLOTTE:
Well, I've always wanted to fly.

JERRY:
There's another plane going down in five days. It gets there the same day as your ship.

CHARLOTTE:
Oh?

JERRY:
Do you know anyone in Buenos Aires?

CHARLOTTE:
No.

JERRY:
It seems a shame to rush down to spend five days alone.

CHARLOTTE:
You'll be busy.

JERRY:
My business can wait. And we did start off for a tour.

CHARLOTTE:
We started off for somewhere.

There is a subtle air of fencing to the above. It is not in the least artful fencing. It is just that they are both being careful not to step too far onto the other's feelings. In fact, their voices would be matter-of-fact if they weren't pitched so low. But there is in his voice, besides matter-of-factness, a quiet entreaty, a pleading.

JERRY:
If I promise to sit at a different table in the dining room and say, "Good morning, Miss Vale, I hope you slept well?" so people will hear me and never guess I'm head over heels in love with you . . . ?

CHARLOTTE (after a long hesitation):
Who am I to quibble over one plane or another?

FADE OUT

FADE IN

121. A HOTEL BALCONY   NIGHT
A velvet, tropical night. Scudding clouds cross the moon,
making changing patterns of light on the balcony. But at
first the balcony is in darkness, for the moon is behind
a large cloud. Only dimly can we discern the figure of
Charlotte, standing by the rail, looking up at the sky.
Then the moon breaks through a slit. She is not alone
on the balcony; Jerry is behind her, by one of the doors
which lead into the rooms. She feels his presence before
she hears him step toward her. She starts swiftly for her
room.

JERRY:
Don't go.

CHARLOTTE:
How did you get here?

JERRY:
Along the balcony. My room is down there. The
whole hotel has gone to bed.

CHARLOTTE:
So must I.

She starts again, but this time he catches her by the hand.

JERRY:
Please! Not yet.

She tries to pull her hand away, but his fingers tighten.

CHARLOTTE:
I'm not going to struggle with you. (Gives up the
struggle.)

JERRY:

That's right. No telling what sort of primitive in-
stincts you might arouse. Cigarette? (She takes one,
he, too. In the matchlight their eyes meet and hers
drop. He offers her his cigarette, lighted.) Friends?

CHARLOTTE:

Yes. (Gives him her cigarette.)

JERRY:

All our lives and after?

CHARLOTTE:

Do you believe in that?

JERRY:

I want to believe that there is a chance for such happiness as this to be carried on somehow, somewhere.

CHARLOTTE:

Are you so happy, then?

JERRY:

Close to it. "Getting warmer and warmer" as we used
to say as children.

CHARLOTTE:

"Look out or it will burn you," *we* used to say.

JERRY:

Are you afraid to get burned if you get too close to
happiness?

CHARLOTTE:

I'm immune to happiness, and so to burns.

JERRY:

You weren't immune the night on the mountain.

CHARLOTTE:

Is that what you call happiness?

JERRY:

> Only a small part. This is, too. Just to stand near you. (Then abruptly; dropping his cigarette.) But, Charlotte! We've only a few days.

CHARLOTTE:

> So wouldn't it be silly? *Nothing.* Gone.

JERRY:

> Like footprints in the snow, leaving no trace when the snow melts.

CHARLOTTE:

> Leaving *nothing.*

JERRY:

> Except what we remember. All our lives—wherever you are, wherever I am. We *are* what our memories are. Whoever gave us this chance to be near each other will give us only one chance. Why, darling, you're crying!

It is the "darling" that finishes her. She leans against him in his arms, sobbing, but her face is averted.

CHARLOTTE:

> They're only tears of gratitude. An old maid's gratitude for the crumbs offered.

JERRY:

> Please don't talk like that.

CHARLOTTE:

> No one ever called me darling before. No even—

JERRY:

> Darling.

He kisses her. Gradually she relaxes, becomes supple, limp, and returns his kiss. Finally:

CHARLOTTE:

> Let me go.

He kisses her again.

122.   THE CIGARETTE IN HER HAND
        falls to the floor.

                                                    FADE OUT

        FADE IN
123.   MOVING SHOT   (STOCK)
        passing the Statue of Liberty. Off-scene, near at hand,
        sound of a blast from the whistle of the cruise ship.

                                                    DISSOLVE TO:

124.   NEW YORK PIER   MED. SHOT   LISA AND JUNE
        are waiting at the foot of a passenger gangplank which
        is being secured. Others crowded around them, also
        waiting for the passengers to come off.

        JUNE (is protesting):
            But what am *I* here for, that's what I want to know!

        LISA:
            To be nice to Charlotte. It won't hurt you for once.

        JUNE:
            To be nice to Aunt Charlotte! To see a poor old maid
            get off a boat! And I simply had a million things to
            do this morning. Or do they matter in the least? A
            ride in the park with Henry, a massage with Mau-
            die, shopping with Helen, and I *faithfully* promised
            Pinkie I'd lunch at the Colony!

        During the above camera pans away to the gangplank.
        Charlotte is the first down. She looks smart, alive, ra-
        diant. Closely following her, hovering attentively, is
        Hamilton Hunneker, carrying her small suitcase, her
        topcoat, his topcoat, and a couple of parcels. Camera
        pans back with them, the timing being such that they
        arrive exactly on the conclusion of June's speech. Nei-
        ther June nor Lisa sees Charlotte until:

        CHARLOTTE:
            Well, here I am! (Kisses Lisa.) Hello, June! (Kisses
            June.)

LISA:
Charlotte! I didn't see you! Charlotte! (They hug.)

June is doing a "double take-em"—this *can't* be Aunt Charlotte.

CHARLOTTE:
Oh—this is Mr. Hunneker. Two more Vales for you, Ham—Missus and Miss.

HAM:
How do?

CHARLOTTE (going right on, to Lisa):
Darling, I got your cable. How's Mother? Not worse?

LISA:
No, no. Charlotte! I can't get over how you *look!*

JUNE (her gape now focused on Ham):
Hamilton Hunneker, *the polo player?*

HAM:
Is that a question, or an accusation?

CHARLOTTE:
Then she isn't *seriously* ill?

Henry Montague, smooth and well groomed, crowds into scene.

MONTIE:
Oh, here are you two beggars. I've got to bustle along. But don't forget our reunion at Glen Cove for the boat races.

CHARLOTTE:
Don't *you* forget.

MONTIE:
Be good, Ham. Say your prayers, Camille. Blessings both, and be sure I'm at the ceremony.

JUNE:
What ceremony?

CHARLOTTE:
> There go the Ricketts. Wave goodbye to the Ricketts,
> Ham. (Waves, calls.) Goodbye!

WOMAN'S VOICE (off):
> Goodbye, Miss Vale! Goodbye, Mr. Hunneker! Be
> sure to look us up in Kansas City!

JUNE:
> Mother! Pinch me!

LISA:
> I'm too busy pinching myself.

CHARLOTTE:
> Ham, dear, you run on.

HAM:
> I'll see you *soon?*

CHARLOTTE:
> I hope so.

Hunneker kisses the palm of her hand, departs. June
gapes. And then Deb and Mack crowd in, forcing us to
pull camera back to make room for them.

DEB:
> Charlotte! We thought we'd lost you! What a jam!

MACK:
> What I say is, now we've found you, we don't *ever*
> intend to lose you.

CHARLOTTE:
> I was going to look you up—(starting an introduc-
> tion.) This is—

But at this moment Mr. Thompson bustles in, too. He
still wears his cruise manager manner, but it is a little
tinged with sadness now that it is almost over.

MR. THOMPSON:
> Don't any of us say goodbye! Not any of us. Just au
> revoir.

CHARLOTTE:
> And this is—Oh, there's too many.

MR. THOMPSON:
> That's right. Skip introductions and skip goodbyes, that's what I always say. Just hello and au revoir. A sad time, isn't it?

CHARLOTTE:
> But it's been fun.

MR. THOMPSON:
> Mainly thanks to you. (To June.) I can tell you one thing, young lady. There was nobody as popular on this cruise as your sister.

JUNE:
> My *sister!*

LISA:
> You'd better clear customs. Come on.

She links her arm with Charlotte's and takes her along. June comes right along, too. Camera trucks ahead into customs shed. Charlotte, looking back, calls her goodbyes to the McIntyres during:

JUNE (to Charlotte):
> Say, what is this! Goodbyes, look us ups, be sures. You could knock me over with a feather.

CHARLOTTE:
> Not with your weight, Roly-Poly.

JUNE:
> Roly-Poly! Where did you get *your* new figure, Auntie dear?

CHARLOTTE:
> There was a doctor in Rio who was very clever.

LISA:
> Keep quiet, June. (To Charlotte.) What's the program for today?

136

CHARLOTTE:

> First Dr. Jaquith. I cabled him to try to save me half an hour.

JUNE:

> Are you going to tell him about your boyfriend?

CHARLOTTE:

> Which one?

JUNE:

> You mean there are *others?*

LISA:

> June, if I were you, I'd give up. (To Charlotte.) Then, *after* the doctor—?

CHARLOTTE:

> Back to Boston . . . I'm flying, at three o'clock. Back to—home. (You can tell she's worried about it.)

LISA (warmly):

> I'll go up with you. June's staying in New York for a few days—

JUNE:

> Not on your life, I'm not! I wouldn't miss the show for the world! I'm going to stand out on the street corner and sell tickets!

> > > > > > DISSOLVE TO:

125. INSERT   THE PLAQUE ON THE BOSTON HOME
"Vale." Charlotte's hand enters scene and rings the bell.

126. MED. SHOT   DRIVEWAY AND FRONT DOOR
The Vale limousine is standing before the front steps. William has driven them from the airport, them meaning Charlotte, Lisa, and June. The latter two are on the back seat, and Lisa is leaning out the opened rear door.

LISA:

> Now, Charlotte, if you prefer, I'll come in with you.

CHARLOTTE:

No, thanks. I'd better do it alone. Just have William drive you home and then bring back my bags.

LISA:

Just as you say. I'll see you tonight, then. Good luck.

CHARLOTTE:

I expect I'll need it.

127.   CLOSER ANGLE   DOORWAY
as it is opened by Dora Pickford, who wears a trained nurse's uniform.

DORA:

Mercy! I heard the car and tried to get down before you rang. I expect you're Miss Charlotte.

128.   REVERSE ANGLE   FROM INSIDE HALL
Charlotte has instantly taken in the uniform and it is apparent that Dora is a stranger to her. As she comes in:

CHARLOTTE:

Yes, I am, but who are—

DORA:

Pickford's my name, Dora, not Mary. I'm the nurse. But we'd better not stand her gabbing. She's got ears like a cat and she heard the bell as sure as preaching.

On this she has led the way down the hall, and there has been nothing for Charlotte to do but follow. Camera trucks ahead of them to the stairs, and then pans them partway up during:

CHARLOTTE:

But wait a minute! Is my mother seriously ill?

DORA:

Fit as a fiddle. Oh, she has a heart—she denies it, but she has one—but then, at her age, who wouldn't have? Nothing serious. It ought to last her years if she doesn't get excited.

CHARLOTTE:
But why didn't someone write? How long has a nurse been necessary?

129. ANGLE FROM FIRST LANDING
as they come up, with Dora chattering glibly on.

DORA:
I wouldn't say a nurse has ever been necessary. Mostly she's used us to fetch and carry. There were three or four others before me. Just in-and-outers. I lasted a whole month. She gave me the sack today, but that's because you're home. You better hurry right in. She'll be waiting and when she waits, she gets mad. And when she gets mad, that means rush the smelling salts. If you need any help, I'll be on the floor above, packing my duds. I left her sitting there all dressed for tonight's party—that is, except for her gown—just as cute as a little red wagon. See you later.

She bounces on up the second flight of stairs. Charlotte looks after her for a minute, rather breathless from the torrent of words. Then she turns toward her mother's door.

130. CLOSE-UP   CHARLOTTE
hesitates before the door. How she hates to go in! But it has to be faced. As she thinks of again meeting her mother, her anger mounts. You can see her getting angrier by the second. Abruptly she reaches for the doorknob, resolved to burst in. But as she reaches halfway, her hand suddenly stops, for all at once she remembers Dr. Jaquith's cautioning words of this afternoon.

DR. JAQUITH'S VOICE:
> Just remember that honoring one's parents is still a
> pretty good idea. You're going to be a shock to her
> and I advise you to soften the blow. Don't throw
> yourself in her face. Give her time to get used to
> you. Remember that whatever she may have done,
> she *is* your mother.

And so Charlotte, instead of bursting in, lightly taps on
the door before she reaches for the knob.

131. INT. MRS. VALE'S ROOM
Mrs. Vale is seated in her high-backed Martha Washington armchair, and she resembles a dowager queen seated
in state on her throne. She wears a white dressing gown
with ostrich feathers. Her transformation, pure white
and glossy as spun glass, rests on her head like a crown.
She wears her pearl-and-diamond dog collar around her
neck, and in her ears pearl-and-diamond earrings. On
her hands, resting on the short arms of the chair, are
large diamonds set in gold. As the door opens and
Charlotte comes in Mrs. Vale turns, and her eyes are
bright, keen, and piercing.

CHARLOTTE:
> Well, Mother, hello! (She swiftly crosses the room,
> leans down, and kisses the surface of the transfor-
> mation.) You're looking wonderfully. Lisa told me
> you haven't been well, but to look at you—

MRS. VALE:
> Step over there where I can see you.

Charlotte hesitates a second, and then obeys. Her
mother lifts her tortoiseshell lorgnette. She is silent for
at least thirty seconds. Then:

MRS. VALE (in an icy tone):
> Turn around. Walk up and down. Take off your hat.
> (Charlotte complies, barely managing to stifle the

old painful self-consciousness.) It's worse than Lisa led me to suppose. Much worse! Much! Much! Much! (She lays her head back and closes her eyes.)

CHARLOTTE:
Mother, if you're feeling ill, I'll get Dora. (Starts toward door.)

MRS. VALE:
Don't go. I have things to say to you. Sit down. (Charlotte comes back, but she takes her time about sitting down.) I have asked a number of the family to dinner at seven thirty—

CHARLOTTE:
Yes, Lisa told me. That's very nice of you, Mother.

MRS. VALE:
There'll be Lloyd and Rosa, Hilary and Justine, Uncle Herbert and Hester, Lisa and June, and also Mr. Elliot Livingston.

CHARLOTTE:
Mr. Livingston is not a member of the family.

MRS. VALE:
Have you rouge on your lips?

CHARLOTTE:
A little.

MRS. VALE:
Have you enamel on your nails?

CHARLOTTE:
A little.

MRS. VALE:
What's happened to your eyebrows?

CHARLOTTE:
Surely you can see.

MRS. VALE:

I think if you wear your glasses tonight, you'll be less of a shock to the others. Also leave off whatever you've got on your face. As to your hair and eyebrows, you can say that often after a severe illness one loses one's hair, and that you are letting yours grow as soon as possible. I am wearing my white lace gown. I'd like you to wear your black and white foulard.

CHARLOTTE:

But, Mother, I've lost over twenty-five pounds—it won't fit.

MRS. VALE:

Oh, yes, it will. I've had Miss Till here for the last week. Hilda, our maid, is just Lisa's size. We fitted all your dresses to her. I've asked Miss Till to stay late tonight in case there is any last-minute alteration necessary.

CHARLOTTE (mutters):

You thought of everything. (She starts for the door once again.)

MRS. VALE:

Wait a minute. I've something else to say to you. Now that you're cured of whatever ailed you and have come home to take up your duties as a daughter again, I have dismissed the last nurse. I have become used to having someone occupying a room on the same floor with me, and in view of my heart, I agree it is a wise precaution. You will occupy your father's room from now on. I had William move all your things down yesterday—your furniture, books, and everything.

CHARLOTTE (coloring resentfully):

You had no right to move my things, Mother.

MRS. VALE:
> No right in my house to move what I see fit? I'm not surprised you blush! I was in the room when William took your books down from the shelves, and let me say that what we found hidden there was a very great shock to me. I can only hope that a shameful episode of your life is completely past.

CHARLOTTE (after a moment; in her old listless tone):
> I think I'll go to my room.

Mrs. Vale watches her, not unkindly, as she goes out.

132.   FIRST FLOOR LANDING
Charlotte closes the door of her mother's room behind her. For a moment she stands looking up the stairway in the direction of her old room, then she listlessly crosses the hall into:

133.   INT. FATHER'S ROOM   CHARLOTTE
comes in. She looks about the room. At first glance she wouldn't know it from her own. Everything has been placed exactly as it had been above, even to the pictures on the walls. There it all is, solid, dull, and inescapable. That is what she is thinking. Tropical waters, the ship, Jerry, Rio, a night on a mountaintop are far away, foolish and unreal. Instead, here is a black and white foulard dress stretched across the bed. She picks up the dress, holds it against her, and looks at herself in a mirror. The dress smells strongly of cleaning fluid which she sniffs distastefully. She sits hopelessly on the bed, letting the dress crumble into her lap.

Hilda comes in through the open hallway door, carrying a florist's small express box. At the sight of Charlotte she stops with a gasp.

CHARLOTTE (with a wry smile):
> Yes, Hilda, it's me.

HILDA:

Welcome home, Miss Charlotte. (Brings over the box.)
This just came. Air Express from New York! (She is
impressed.)

CHARLOTTE:

It must have come up on the same plane with me.
(She takes the box and examines it with curiosity
and surprise, examines the tag.)

HILDA:

Miss Till is here about the dress. Do you want her
in?

CHARLOTTE:

In a little while.

HILDA:

Yes, Miss.

She exits. Charlotte undoes the box, removes the brown
paper, the several layers of newspaper beneath, raises
the cover and lifts out a cotton batting wrapped bundle.
She unbinds the cotton batting, revealing a corsage of
red camellias. There is no card, but there is no need for
a card. All at once the Boston world is unreal and the
world of Jerry and Camille—the world that was lost—
is the only reality. He hasn't forgotten. In the moment
she has needed him most, he has sent her this wordless
message. Her hands tremble as she picks up the flowers. Camera moves to a close-up of the camellias.

DISSOLVE TO:

134. A FLASHBACK

It takes place in a corner of the Pan American airport at
Rio. Through a window the Clipper can be seen moored
to a long runway which juts out into Rio Harbor.

But at first the scene is a close-up of two branches of
camellias which are being passed from Jerry's hands to
Charlotte's. She raises the blooms up and camera pulls
back just enough to form a close-up of her. As she looks

at the flowers, her eyes slowly fill with tears. Then she looks up and the angle widens just enough to include Jerry. We see now that they are standing by the window, and through it we see the Clipper, with its engines warming up.

JERRY:

I got them from a vendor outside. I was lucky.

His voice is very quiet and just a little choked. She looks down at the flowers again.

CHARLOTTE:

I hate goodbyes! I hate last anythings. Last acts, last words, last minutes!

JERRY:

The last words of a book only say "the end." That doesn't alter the character of the book—it's what's gone before that matters.

CHARLOTTE:

And what can't go afterward.

JERRY:

Sometime we may see each other . . .

CHARLOTTE:

No! We promised. We both solemnly promised. We have done nothing wrong. But then it would seem wrong—shameful and guilty. I couldn't endure that—deceit—the pangs of conscience. We were both to just go home—and live out the rest of our lives in our own particular garrets.

JERRY:

Will it help you to know that my own garret will be more endurable because you have furnished it with beautiful things?

CHARLOTTE:

And mine, Jerry! And mine!

A sharp three bells from off-scene and then:

A VOICE (first in Portuguese, then in English):
>   Passengers on board!

JERRY:
>   Goodbye! (They kiss and cling to each other for a moment.)

CHARLOTTE:
>   Goodbye!

DISSOLVE TO:

THE CLIPPER
taking off.

DISSOLVE TO:

JERRY'S FACE
as he watches the plane soar into the air, his head turning.[10]

DISSOLVE TO:

135.   INSERT   THE CAMELLIAS
Camera pans up to a mirror in which we see the reflection of Charlotte.

136.   INT. CHARLOTTE'S ROOM   CHARLOTTE
is standing before a mirror applying Jolies Fleurs from the bottle Jerry gave her. She wears a dressing gown, is ready for dinner except for her dress. On the dressing table beside her are Jerry's camellias. Camera pulls back. Hilda is in the room, making up the bed. Charlotte has not bothered to have her own furniture moved back in— she will use her father's. And she has not had the horrible pictures brought back. Her baggage is here and partially unpacked.

HILDA:
>   I'll bring your clothes up as soon as ever I get a chance.

CHARLOTTE:
>   No, thank you, Hilda. You may leave them down in the other room. I shan't need them anymore.

Hilda registers surprise, but is prevented from answering by the sudden entrance of Mrs. Vale, who comes in
without knocking and stops in the doorway. Mrs. Vale
is dressed for dinner and she carries her cane. Charlotte
sees her, in fact, looks in her direction for a moment,
and then goes on with what she was doing.

MRS. VALE:
> What are you doing in this room?

CHARLOTTE:
> Getting ready to sleep here. (Her tone is light, even
> playfully cajoling.)

MRS. VALE (to Hilda):
> You may go.

HILDA:
> Yes, ma'am! (She scuttles out.)

MRS. VALE:
> Didn't you understand I wish someone to sleep on
> the same floor with me?

CHARLOTTE:
> We'll ask one of the maids. Or perhaps we can get
> the nurse to come back.

MRS. VALE:
> We! So long as I pay the bills, I am running this house.
> Please remember you are my guest, Charlotte.

CHARLOTTE:
> Then please treat me like one. Your guest prefers to
> sleep in this room, if you don't mind.

MRS. VALE (points at the flowers with her stick):
> Where did these come from?

CHARLOTTE:
> From New York.

MRS. VALE:
> Who sent them?

CHARLOTTE:

I forget the name of the florist. Here's the tag. (She gets the tag and offers it to her mother, who waves it aside.)

MRS. VALE:

I've seen it. I had the box brought to me first. You know perfectly well what I mean. What *person* sent the flowers?

CHARLOTTE:

There wasn't any card.

MRS. VALE:

In other words, you don't intend to tell me.

Charlotte steps behind a screen, taking with her a dress. Out of sight, she puts it on during:

CHARLOTTE:

Mother, I don't want to be unkind or disagreeable. I've come home to live with you again, here in the same house. But it can't be in the same way. I've been living my own life, making my own decisions for a long while now. I don't think I will do anything of importance that will displease you, but, Mother, from now on you must give me complete freedom— including deciding where I sleep, what I read, what I wear— (She steps out from behind the screen. Her dinner dress is smartly, somewhat daringly cut. She is zippering it.)

MRS. VALE:

Where did you get that dress?

CHARLOTTE:

Lisa and I bought it in New York today.

MRS. VALE:

It's outrageous. Where is the black and white foulard?

CHARLOTTE (has stepped to dresser, is recombing her hair):
> I gave it to Miss Till. She was most grateful. Mother, please be fair and meet me halfway.

MRS. VALE:
> They told me before you were born that my recompense for a late child was the comfort the child would be to me in my old age, especially if it was a girl. And on your first day home after a six months' absence, you act like this!

CHARLOTTE:
> I'll be ready to go down as soon as I pin on my flowers. (Starts to pin them on.)

MRS. VALE:
> I prefer to go down alone, thank you. (Exits.)

CHARLOTTE:
> Just as you wish.

137. CLOSE-UP OF CHARLOTTE
as she pins on the flowers. She is feeling no sense of triumph, but only a regret that her mother has been unwilling to compromise.

138. HALLWAY OUTSIDE CHARLOTTE'S ROOM
Mrs. Vale, filled with righteous indignation, starts down the stairs, using the cane. When two or three steps down, she stops and looks back toward Charlotte's room as if she means to go back and carry on the quarrel. But Charlotte at that moment appears in the doorway and she decides against it. She turns again to go downstairs.

139. INSERT STEP
The untipped point of the cane strikes the hardwood surface of the step just beside the stair runner. The cane slips, flies up.

140.   CLOSE-UP OF CHARLOTTE
as her face registers what she sees, her mother falling.
Sound of a crash and her mother's body rolling downstairs.

CHARLOTTE (screams):
Mother! (She runs forward out of scene, past camera.)

141.   ANGLE FROM FIRST LANDING
In foreground Mrs. Vale is lying in a heap at the foot of
the stairs. Charlotte runs down as fast as she can. A
second later Dora comes out of a door at the head of the
stairs and runs down, too.

DORA:
Coming!

Charlotte reaches the foot of the stairs and kneels beside
her mother.

DORA (running down):
Don't touch her. Let *me*. Here I am! I heard it all.

CHARLOTTE (looks up at her):
If I've killed her—But Mrs. Vale has begun to moan.

DORA:
Don't worry. If she can moan like that, she's good
and alive. Just run call a doctor. There's one right
down the street—Dr. Regan. He's cute.
                                        DISSOLVE TO:

142.   INT. MRS. VALE'S ROOM   CLOSE-UP   MRS. VALE
in bed, her face ashen and drawn with pain.

143.   WIDER ANGLE   TO INCLUDE DR. REGAN, CHARLOTTE,
DORA, AND HILDA
gathered about the bed. Dan Regan, the doctor, young,
rather handsome, is taping up Mrs. Vale's ankle.

CHARLOTTE (whispers to him):
   Is she conscious?

DAN (with a grin):
   If she's not, it's the darndest torn ligament I've ever encountered. It will swell and discolor. She mustn't walk on it.

CHARLOTTE:
   I feel responsible. We had a quarrel—

MRS. VALE (opens her eyes):
   Charlotte, I believe there are dinner guests waiting downstairs. Or have you discarded your manners, too?

CHARLOTTE:
   But, mother, hadn't I better—

MRS. VALE:
   You may tell my family that they may come up to see me one or two at a time.

Dan touches Charlotte's arm, gestures with his head for her to step aside with him. Camera pans with them.

DAN:
   Go right ahead with your plans.

CHARLOTTE:
   Are you sure—?

DAN:
   In my opinion the old lady's—I beg your pardon— I think your mother is enjoying the excitement she's going to cause.

MRS. VALE'S VOICE:
   Must you whisper? Am I to have no attention at all?

Dan winks at Charlotte and opens the door for her.

144.   HALLWAY OUTSIDE MRS. VALE'S ROOM
Charlotte comes out and starts downstairs.

145. **STAIRWAY FROM LOWER HALL   CHARLOTTE**
comes down. She can hear the indistinguishable talk from the drawing room now. The family! Even before the prospect of meeting them she hesitates. But she touches Jerry's flowers. They are an amulet. She straightens and walks out into:

146. **INT. DRAWING ROOM   CHARLOTTE**
appears from the hallway and stops.

> **CHARLOTTE:**
> Hello, everybody. (In a voice she forces to sound casual.)

147. **REVERSE ANGLE   PAST HER TOWARD THE FAMILY**
Six heads turn and stare—Lloyd and Rosa, Hilary and Justine, Uncle Herbert and Hester. Their faces are a study in arrested motion. As for Elliot Livingston, he is looking with a sort of startled interest. Lisa's eyes are dancing from one astounded face to another; she is hugely enjoying the moment. June is the first to move or speak. She rushes up to Charlotte, as if proud of her prerogative, slips her arm through hers.

> **JUNE:**
> You're gorgeous! I simply love your dress. (Leads her into room.)

> **CHARLOTTE:**
> Thank you, June. (Camera follows Charlotte as she goes first to Aunt Hester and Uncle Herbert.) Aunt Hester! How are you? (Kisses her cheek.)

> **AUNT HESTER** (too aghast for words):
> Well—!

> **UNCLE HERBERT:**
> Well—!

CHARLOTTE (says it for him):
> "By Jove!" (Kisses his cheek, passes on.) Rosa, I'm
> *glad* to see you.

ROSA:
> Why, Charlotte—

CHARLOTTE (again says it):
> "How you've changed." (Business of kissing hers and
> Lloyd's cheeks.) But you haven't, Lloyd, I'm happy
> to say. (Passes on toward Justine and Hilary.)

JUSTINE:
> I couldn't be more astonished.

CHARLOTTE:
> Yes, it was a shock, wasn't it? (Business of kissing
> cheeks.) But the doctor says it's only a torn liga-
> ment. You *did* mean Mother, didn't you?

HILARY:
> Why—naturally she meant Mother.

CHARLOTTE:
> Brother dear . . .

She passes on. Lisa puts her arm around her.

LISA (whispers):
> How did it go?

CHARLOTTE (whispers):
> I don't know. I think I won the first round.

LISA (aloud):
> Do you know Elliot Livingston?

CHARLOTTE (cordially acknowledges the introduction):
> How do you do?

ELLIOT:
> How do you do? (He is visibly impressed.)

153

CHARLOTTE (to William, who comes in):
William, I think we'll have some cocktails if you can find a recipe book. (And then noting the general reaction, adds.) And you'd better bring the sherry, too.

JUNE (puts in):
Where did you get the flowers, Aunt Charlotte? Ham Hunnecker, I guess.

CHARLOTTE (winks at her):
Guess again, Roly-Poly.

ELLIOT:
Will you tell me why we never met before?

CHARLOTTE:
The world is a small place, but Boston is a big one.

ELLIOT:
By gad, that's right.

CHARLOTTE (to all):
Does anybody else notice a chill in this room? Let's have a fire. (Goes to fireplace.)

JUSTINE (aghast):
You don't mean an open fire!

HILARY (warns):
No, no, Charlotte! Mother won't like it.

CHARLOTTE:
That reminds me. She asked for you to come up by ones and twos. Uncle Herbert, you're the oldest. You'd better go first.

LLOYD:
Be careful, Charlotte. For as long as I can remember, that fire has never been lit.

CHARLOTTE (gaily):
　High time it was, then!

She has already stooped and lighted a match. Elliot hurries to her and reaches for it.

ELLIOT:
　May I help you?

CHARLOTTE:
　Thank you.

As he applies the match, the white paper fans, yellowed with age, blaze up.

148.　THE FIREPLACE
with the fire almost burned out.

149.　HALLWAY AT FRONT DOOR　GENERAL SHOT
People are leaving. Lloyd and Rosa are calling their final good nights from just outside the door. Hilary and Justine are having their cheeks kissed by Charlotte and are kissing back in return this time. Lisa, June, and Elliot are waiting their turn. Uncle Herbert and Hester are upstairs. There is a general air of cordiality which is in marked contrast to the atmosphere before dinner.

JUSTINE (is saying):
　I had no idea you played bridge, Charlotte. Are you doing anything Wednesday for lunch and afterward? I'm short a player—and if you think Mother will spare you—

CHARLOTTE:
　I'd love to come, Justine, if you think I'll fit in.

JUSTINE:
　I think you'd fit in anywhere. And furthermore, I think—

CHARLOTTE:
No more, Justine, or I shall cry. Good night.

As they go on,

LISA (whispers):
I'm proud. Dr. Jaquith would be, too.

Charlotte just squeezes her.

JUNE:
Aunt Charlotte, can you ever forgive me?

CHARLOTTE:
Never!

And she hugs her and each of them sniffles a little.

HILARY (from door):
Are you coming, Elliot?

ELLIOT:
Just a minute. (Then to Charlotte as she offers her hand.) I still can't get over our not having met.

CHARLOTTE:
As a matter of fact, we have. Once and almost twice.

ELLIOT:
I'm mystified.

CHARLOTTE:
When we were children, you were the only boy who ever danced with me at dancing school. (Then, before he can answer, adds.) And the "almost" was when you were supposed to usher at my coming-out party and didn't show up.

ELLIOT:
I'm covered with shame.

CHARLOTTE:
I shouldn't have told you. It wasn't nice.

ELLIOT:

    Well, I hope you're going to allow me to make up for my past rudeness. May I telephone you some-time?

CHARLOTTE:

    Any time, of course. Good night, Mr. Livingston.

She shuts the door after him and exits scene toward back of hall.

150.   ANGLE TOWARD STAIRWAY   UNCLE HERBERT AND AUNT HESTER

are coming down. Charlotte, entering, meets them near the lower steps.

UNCLE HERBERT (sternly):

    She wants to see you at once.

CHARLOTTE:

    Then I'll hurry. Good night. Can you let yourselves out?

Quick kisses.

AUNT HESTER:

    Yes, indeed.

UNCLE HERBERT:

    And thank you for a most—unusual evening.

Camera goes up with Charlotte. Dora comes out of Mrs. Vale's room and runs to meet her halfway.

DORA:

    She wants—

CHARLOTTE:

    Yes, I know, to see me at once.

DORA:

    She's had two hours' sleep and she's bright as a but-ton. And mad! Of course she smelled the fire and

sent Hilda to investigate. You'd better just let her
blow off her steam. I've put two tablespoons of sherry
and a sleeping powder in her hot milk, so it shouldn't
last long. I'll wait right outside the door.

CHARLOTTE:
Dora, I suspect you're a treasure.

She goes into:

151.   INT. MRS. VALES'S ROOM   MRS. VALE AND CHARLOTTE
as latter enters. Mrs. Vale is in bed, lying flat on her
back, the bedclothes pulled up to her chin, her elevated
foot making a towering mound under the pink silk blan-
ket cover. There is a low light in a far corner. Mrs. Vale's
head lies in the dark shadow cast by the high footboard,
but Charlotte can see, outlined on the pillow, the transformation, which at this time of night indicates her
mother's moods. And beneath it, the two phosphores-
cent sparks of her eyes.

CHARLOTTE:
How is the ankle, Mother?

MRS. VALE:
Extremely painful.

CHARLOTTE:
I'm so sorry. But it's splendid you've had some good
sleep.

MRS. VALE:
I haven't closed my eyes. I've been doing some
thinking—as I've been lying here in pain, listening
to you all having a good time downstairs. How much
did that dress cost?

CHARLOTTE:
It was frightfully expensive. I'll tell you in the morning.

MRS. VALE:

To whom did you charge it?

CHARLOTTE:

To whom I've always charged my clothes, Mother.

MRS. VALE:

And do you expect me to pay for articles charged to me of which I do not approve?

CHARLOTTE:

I'll pay for it out of my own account. I've saved for years. I have almost five thousand dollars.

MRS. VALE:

Five thousand dollars won't last long. Especially if your monthly allowance should be discontinued.

There is a pause. So this is what Mother has wanted to get off her chest.

CHARLOTTE:

Oh. When Father set up a trust for the boys, why didn't he make one for me, too?

MRS. VALE:

Because he wisely left your affairs to my own better judgement. I'm sure you've always had everything in the world you want.

CHARLOTTE:

I haven't had independence.

MRS. VALE:

That's it! That's just what I want to talk about! Independence—to buy what you choose, wear what you choose, sleep where you choose, light fires in my fireplaces if you choose! Independence! That's what you mean by it, isn't it?

CHARLOTTE:

Dr. Jaquith says independence is reliance upon one's own will and judgement.

MRS. VALE:

I make the decisions here, Charlotte. I am willing that you occupy your old room until I dismiss the nurse. She will occupy your father's room for the time being and perform a daughter's duties as well as a nurse's. That will give you a good chance to think over what I have said. I am glad to give a devoted daughter a home under my roof and pay all her expenses, but not if she scorns my authority.

CHARLOTTE:

I could earn my own living. I think I'd make a very good headwaitress in a restaurant.

MRS. VALE:

You may think that's very funny, but I guess you'd be laughing out of the other side of your face if I actually did carry out my suggestion.

CHARLOTTE:

No, I don't think I would. I'm not afraid. (She stops abruptly. What has she said? She repeats it.) I'm not afraid! Mother, I'm not afraid![11] (The wonder of it fills her with a sort of radiance.)

MRS. VALE:

Where's Dora? I want Dora. (She raises her hand and knocks with her wedding ring against the headboard. Instantly Dora appears.) I want the back of my head rubbed, and my ankle rebandaged, and my pillows fixed, and another cup of that hot toddy.

DORA:

Which first, Queen Elizabeth?

MRS. VALE:

Head rubbed. (As Dora complies.) That's good. Don't stop. You're a good girl, Dora. You're a good, devoted girl. Guess *you* wouldn't stick up your nose at a fortune, would you, Dora? (Her voice is thick with sleep now.)

DORA:
> You're groggy, Granny dear, and talking perfect nonsense. Nobody's listening. Charlotte's gone up to bed.

She winks one eye at Charlotte and the latter slips quietly out of the room. On the old, sleepy, somewhat defeated but still formidable face of Mrs. Vale,

FADE OUT

FADE IN

152. INT. CHARLOTTE'S ROOM   CLOSE-UP   PRINT OF A CAMEL-LIA
Charlotte's hands are in scene, cutting it down with scissors to postcard size. She fits it into an envelope, turns the envelope over, and writes:

J. D. DURRANCE, ESQ.

Then, as she starts to add the address, she stops, her pen suspended. A pause, then:

CHARLOTTE'S VOICE (but slightly altered for the effect):
> You can't send it to his office. *Her* cousin is his secretary. Suppose she opens his mail? (Camera pulls back. Charlotte is seated at her writing desk. A window at her back shows the snow still falling. Charlotte meditates, now tapping her teeth with the end of the pen.) Well, she wouldn't know anything—it's only a picture. (Then, answering herself.) But she'd guess. Anyone would. The whole thing reeks of romantic sentimentality. Might as well send him a valentine!

About to put down the pen, she gets an idea. She reaches for a sheet of writing paper and begins to write rapidly. For a moment we wonder what this move means. Then:

153. INSERT   LETTER
She has already written:

Dear Deb:

How are you and how is Mack? I think of you, miss you. Why don't you ever come to Boston? We could talk over our trip and the fun we had together.

Which reminds me, do you ever see Jerry?

CHARLOTTE'S VOICE (scornfully):
Very subtle, Miss Vale.

Next time you do, you might say hello for me

CHARLOTTE'S VOICE:
He'll know the rest.

And if it isn't too much trouble, please give him the enclosed envelope. I seem to have forgotten his address.

CHARLOTTE'S VOICE:
That's a lie. You know it forward and backward. You know his telephone number, too, but you daren't use it.

There's nothing much in it, just an old flower print. He has a hobby for collecting them, he told me, and this is a rather special one I happened to see . . .

FADE OUT

FADE IN

154.   INT. DR. JAQUITH'S NEW YORK OFFICE
INSERT   AN ENVELOPE
It is addressed to:

Dr. Henry Jaquith
64th & Bell Streets
New York City.

Dr. Jaquith's hand turns over the envelope and we read on the back: Miss C. Vale, Boston, Mass. And with a letter opener, the doctor's hands slit open the envelope. Camera pulls back to a close shot of Dr. Jaquith seated in a chair in his office. He reads the letter and as he does so, we hear:

CHARLOTTE'S VOICE:
Dear Dr. Jaquith: Summer, winter, and now spring again. I won't say time flies, but it doesn't crawl as it used to do. Between Mother and me there is still an armed truce. She threatens, but she doesn't act. I follow your advice: I stick by my guns but don't fire. (Dr. Jaquith's nod registers his approval.) There is a man here who has been nice to me. In fact, he has proposed to me and there are no arguments I can think of why I should not marry him. Most every woman wants a man of her own—a home of her own and a child of her own. His name is Elliot Livingston. He is from a fine Boston family and is a fine man, too. A widower with two half-grown sons. I don't know why I tell you this except that I tell you almost everything . . . [12]

DISSOLVE TO:

155.   INT. MRS. VALE'S ROOM   CLOSE SHOT   A BOX OF RED ROSES
Charlotte's hand comes in, takes out a card. Camera pulls back. Charlotte is dressed for the evening in another new dress. As she opens the card Mrs. Vale watches her intently from the wheelchair in which these days she is confined.

MRS. VALE:
Well, I can't *force* you to tell me who they're from.

CHARLOTTE:
Elliot.

MRS. VALE:
Why haven't you accepted him? Do you imagine a *Livingston* is waiting for you on every corner?

CHARLOTTE (teasing):
Well, I've been waiting to know how *you* feel about it.

MRS. VALE:

> You know as well as I do that it doesn't make a bit
> of difference to you how I feel about it. You'll do
> exactly as you please anyway.

Her eyes are shining with the zest of combat. The cor-
ners of her mouth are twitching, but not with anger.

CHARLOTTE:

> Mother, you're glad! You're pleased!

MRS. VALE:

> I'm no such thing. I'm only astonished that of all of
> the family you should bring such a feather to the
> family cap.

CHARLOTTE:

> Well then, if you really do approve—Mother dear—

MRS. VALE (pushing her away):

> Better save all that soft talk for your Elliot.

A tap on the door. As Charlotte goes to answer it:

CHARLOTTE:

> There's no one like you, Mother! And all these years
> I haven't given you any sort of a game![13]

It is Hilda at the door.

HILDA:

> Mr. Livingston is waiting.

CHARLOTTE:

> Thank you, Hilda. Will you bring a vase for the
> flowers? And leave them here for Mother. (Then to
> Mrs. Vale.) Don't wait up. It's dinner and a concert.

MRS. VALE (as Charlotte exits):

> I'll wait up if I wish to wait up!

156.   LOWER HALL AND STAIRWAY

As Charlotte comes down Elliot is waiting. Under his

overcoat he wears full evening dress and carries his hat. William is waiting at the foot of the stairs with a small florist's box.

CHARLOTTE:
Hello! Wouldn't they let you sit down?

ELLIOT:
We're a little late. You're looking lovely.

CHARLOTTE:
Thank you—and for the roses. They're beautiful.

WILLIAM:
This just came from the florist, miss. (Hands her box.)

CHARLOTTE:
All right, William. We'll let ourselves out.

WILLIAM:
Yes, miss.

From the box she takes a corsage of camellias. William exits. As Charlotte and Elliot go to the front door, while she pins on the camellias:

ELLIOT:
And yet you wear camellias. Why do you always, Charlotte?

CHARLOTTE (lightly):
Just a personal idiosyncrasy. We're all entitled to them.

ELLIOT:
And yet you never let me buy them. Why don't you?

157.   EXT. HOUSE
as Charlotte and Elliot come out. His chauffeur-driven limousine is waiting.

CHARLOTTE:
Aren't you full of questions.

ELLIOT:
And aren't you full of mystery.

CHARLOTTE:
I?

They get into the car.

158. INT. CAR   CLOSE SHOT   ELLIOT AND CHARLOTTE
The chauffeur closes the car door. Elliot rolls up the glass partition between their section and the chauffeur as he continues.

ELLIOT:
Not just your taste in flowers. Deeper, much. There's something about you, yourself, that I can't get hold of. You put me off and don't tell me why. I don't even know if you're thinking favorably or unfavorably.

CHARLOTTE:
Favorably, Elliot.

The car is in motion now.

ELLIOT:
I haven't wanted to rush you off your feet—I've been patient.

CHARLOTTE:
You've been a dear. But, Elliot, there are so many things to think about . . . To step into another woman's domain—take over her house—and her sons—

ELLIOT:
You can redo the house. Or I'll build you a new one. It was my mother and sisters who told me how difficult it would be for you.

CHARLOTTE:
Have you discussed me with your mother and sisters?

166

ELLIOT:
>Oh yes—and my sons, too. I did everything before I spoke to you.

159.   CLOSE-UP   CHARLOTTE

CHARLOTTE'S VOICE:
>Except make love to me. (She has grown silent, meditative.)

160.   BACK TO TWO-SHOT
as he notices her mood.

ELLIOT:
>What are you thinking?

CHARLOTTE (a little startled):
>Oh . . . (Then chooses a thought.) Elaine was a very wonderful girl. Do you often think of her?

ELLIOT:
>Well, yes. I want to be honest. But you needn't be afraid that Elaine will ever come back in any way. She's just a memory now, like—

CHARLOTTE:
>Footprints in the snow.

ELLIOT:
>Eh?

CHARLOTTE:
>No. Much more substantial. You have her sons—the countless things she has touched and are part of her.

CHARLOTTE'S VOICE:
>And I have only a dried corsage and an empty bottle of perfume and I can't even say his name!

ELLIOT (misunderstanding her wistfulness):
>All I want to make you understand is that I shall begin a new life with you and for you.

CHARLOTTE:
> I wonder if we had a child which one of us it would resemble.

ELLIOT (startled):
> A child?

CHARLOTTE:
> Now I've shocked you. (Then lightly.) But, nevertheless, when I marry you, that will be one of the chief reasons.

ELLIOT:
> Well, whatever the reason, if you don't do it soon—

Charlotte takes the plunge—lightly—afraid that if she stops to be serious, she will change her mind.

CHARLOTTE:
> I didn't say "if," Elliot. I said "when."

ELLIOT:
> You mean—? Charlotte. Charlotte, dear.

She looks up at him and smiles. Then he kisses her reverently.

DISSOLVE TO:

161.   INT. WESTON DRAWING ROOM
The butler has just shown in Charlotte and Elliot from the hallway. George Weston and his wife, Gracie, Elliot's sister, are welcoming them.

GRACIE:
> Charlotte, dear! Elliot, you're bad.

ELLIOT:
> I know we're late. Hello, George.

CHARLOTTE:
> It was my fault.

GEORGE:
> "Last the best," as we used to say. But come on, let's find a cocktail. I'm a couple up on you.

During this, Gracie has taken Elliot into the room, and
now George brings Charlotte in, camera trucking ahead
of them.

GEORGE:
> Let me see. I think we have Martinis and old-
> fashioneds. Which for you?

CHARLOTTE:
> It doesn't—

Suddenly she stops, and almost stops walking, too.

162. FROM HER PERSPECTIVE   IN THE CROWD AT THE FAR END
OF THE ROOM   JERRY
is talking to a couple of women.

163. BACK TO CHARLOTTE AND GEORGE

GEORGE:
> What's the matter? See a ghost?

CHARLOTTE:
> No, nothing. I think I know that man talking to
> Hortense and Barbara. I think he was on a boat with
> me once.

GEORGE:
> J. D.? Durrance. He's doing a job for me—architect
> for the medical center.

CHARLOTTE:
> He's an *architect?*

GEORGE:
> Um. Nice chap. Not Boston, but all right. When
> Gracie was short a man for tonight, I remembered
> he was coming up, gave him a ring, and told him to
> throw in some evening clothes. We've been trying
> to get him to dinner all winter. Shall I tell him your
> name or let him guess?

CHARLOTTE:
Let him guess.

Two or three steps in silence bring them to J. D.

GEORGE:
Here's somebody who thinks she's met you before,
J. D.

When Jerry turns and faces Charlotte, his face is set in
a formal smile. For an instant it undergoes complete
change. But then neither his manner nor voice betrays
any of the emotions which Charlotte has seen registered on his face in that flash.

JERRY:
Why, yes, of course! (He says shaking hands.) You
do look familiar. Don't tell me her name, George.
Wait a minute, I've got it. Beauchamp, isn't it? Camille Beauchamp. Am I right?

GEORGE (laughing):
Sorry, J. D. This is not the same lady . . .

CHARLOTTE:
Vale is my name. I met you on a pleasure cruise once.

JERRY:
Oh, yes, Miss Vale. I hope you'll forgive me. I'm
sure I—

GEORGE (to the others):
Let's leave it to him to make his own peace.

He takes the women away and Charlotte and Jerry are
left alone. But not quite alone. The crowd is still about
and they are careful.

CHARLOTTE:
George tells me you've been in Boston quite often
this winter, Mr. Durrance. (And I didn't know!)

JERRY:
Yes, several times. (You're looking simply glorious!)

CHARLOTTE:
> You're an architect? (I could cry with pride!)

JERRY:
> Yes. It's an interesting job I'm doing for George. (I've wanted horribly to call you up!)

CHARLOTTE:
> The medical center, he tells me. (An architect!)

JERRY:
> Yes. (I've walked by your house on Marlborough Street. Once I almost rang the bell.)

CHARLOTTE (as the butler brings cocktails):
> Do you ever hear anything from Mack and Deb McIntyre? You introduced them to me on the trip, do you remember?

JERRY:
> They're both in fine feather, last time I saw them.

CHARLOTTE:
> And how is Tina?

JERRY:
> Well, Tina—(His face clouds.) We're have a pretty bad time with Tina.

CHARLOTTE:
> Tell me about it.

JERRY:
> I'm afraid we've got to send her away somewhere. The doctor thinks she shouldn't be with her mother. I took her to talk to Dr. Jaquith. He was highly recommended to me by this Camille Beauchamp I mistook you for. (Oh, Camille, Camille! I'm still horribly in love!)

164. WIDER ANGLE   GROUP   INCLUDING GRACIE
who calls out.

GRACIE:
>   Come on, everybody. We'll have to dine now or we'll
>   never get to the concert.

DISSOLVE TO:

165.   INT. CONCERT HALL   CLOSE TRUCKING SHOT
Slowly moving in to Elliot, then continuing to include
Charlotte, then continuing to go past Elliot and include
Charlotte and Jerry. The orchestra is playing. Elliot is
seated on the aisle. As camera goes past him and Charlotte, we see that he is holding her hand, his fingers
interlocked with hers. He is looking at the stage. She is
looking at him at first, and then down at their hands.
And then she looks to the other side at Jerry as camera
moves on. Jerry is also staring straight at the stage. For
a long moment Charlotte looks at him, and one can tell
that the feelings that should be flowing toward Elliot are
running unstemmed in the other direction. After a moment:

JERRY (without looking, whispers):
>   Don't look at me like that. I can't hear a thing as it
>   is. Can you?

CHARLOTTE (whispers):
>   No.

She looks at the stage. Then Jerry looks at her. After a
moment his look leaves her face and goes to the camellias she is wearing. She looks at them, too.

JERRY:
>   Camille! (She only half looks at him.) I've got to see
>   you!

CHARLOTTE:
>   Yes!

JERRY:
>   I leave for New York on the one o'clock train. May I
>   come to your house tonight? I won't stay but ten
>   minutes. I must talk to you.

CHARLOTTE:
> Yes, come.

DISSOLVE TO:

166.   EXT. CHARLOTTE'S HOUSE
Elliot is letting her out of the car.

CHARLOTTE:
> I'm a little tired. Please don't stay tonight, Elliot.

ELLIOT:
> Of course not, dear. (Kisses her.) Is anything the matter?

CHARLOTTE:
> No, Elliot. Just tired. I'll be all right in the morning. Good night.

She pats his hand and, camera panning, runs into the house.

167.   INT. HALLWAY   CHARLOTTE
comes in. She drops her evening coat on a chair and goes into:

168.   INT. THE DRAWING ROOM
It is unlighted. Charlotte goes to the front windows. She pulls aside the heavy draperies and raises the window shade. Elliot's car is just going out the driveway.

169.   CLOSE-UP   CHARLOTTE   THROUGH THE WINDOW
as she sets herself to wait for Jerry.

170.   INSERT   CLOCK IN HALL
which shows the time to be 11:30.

DISSOLVE TO:

171.   CLOCK IN DRAWING ROOM OVER FIREPLACE
with the time indicated as 12:35. Pan over to Charlotte, at the window, still waiting. She is both puzzled and

173

hurt at Jerry's failure to come. After a moment she leaves the window and walks out into:

172.   HALLWAY   CHARLOTTE
comes in from drawing room. As she is starting for the stairway, walking slowly, the telephone rings. She hurries to it. Camera moves up to her during:

CHARLOTTE:
Hello . . . Jerry, you said—I've been waiting!

173.   INT. TELEPHONE BOOTH IN BOSTON BACK BAY
STATION   JERRY
is at the phone.

JERRY:
Yes, I know. I purposely left it for the last minute to call you.
(INTERCUT):

CHARLOTTE:
But *why*, Jerry—?

JERRY:
On the way home from the theater Mrs. Weston told me the news. You're engaged to marry her brother.

CHARLOTTE:
I wanted to tell you.

JERRY:
I shouldn't have asked to see you. I knew I shouldn't, but I didn't know. I just didn't know!

CHARLOTTE:
Where are you? Which station? Back Bay, isn't it? Wait for me. I'll come to you!

And on his protest:

JERRY:

> No, Charlotte, you—

She hangs up. Camera panning, she snatches up her coat and runs out the front door.

WIPE OFF TO:

174.   BACK BAY RAILWAY STATION   WAITING PLATFORM
Charlotte comes down the steps from the upper level. She looks about, sees him, hurries out.

175.   JERRY
has not seen her yet. In the background, not too near, a redcap waits with his suitcase. Then Jerry does see her as she hurries towrd him and, as she enters scene:

JERRY:

> You shouldn't have come. If someone sees you—

CHARLOTTE:

> I don't care! I have to tell you—

JERRY:

> Why are you marrying the Livingston? Do you love him?

His voice is harsh and grating, not like Jerry's at all.

CHARLOTTE:

> Not as we do. Not like us. I thought in time it might grow to be, or something like it. I thought I was getting over you, Jerry. You were fading a little, as you said you would. I didn't think I'd ever see you again. We made our pact and you were keeping it. I sent you the picture of the camellia through Deb and Mack, and when you didn't reply, I thought—

JERRY:

> I didn't get your picture. But never mind about that now. What sort of man is this Livingston?

CHARLOTTE:

Like you in lots of ways. That's one reason why I thought I could care for him in time. Oh, not your sense of humor, nor your sense of beauty, nor sense of play . . . But a fine man—and a refuge I thought I could never have.

JERRY:

Of course!

CHARLOTTE:

Are you angry with me?

JERRY:

No. Only with myself. The old-fashioned word "cad" is about right for a man who makes a woman like you care for him, and then, because of some noble sense of duty, leaves her to get over it the best she can . . . It was inexcusable enough even when it began. I knew I was getting in pretty deep, but when I assured you it would be just an episode soon over and completely over, I was fooling myself. It's been nearly a year and I can't forget you, Charlotte.

CHARLOTTE:

I know! Don't I know!

JERRY:

And there's not a thing I can do about it. Not a thing! Isobel depends on me more and more. She's ill and getting worse and I'm all she's got. Then there's Tina. She'll be waiting for me at the end of the train shed in New York when I get in. She's got some sort of phobia that I'm going to die or run off and leave her. And even if I could chuck everything, Charlotte—

CHARLOTTE:

I wouldn't let you!

His train comes in with a roar, robbing them for an interval of any chance to speak, at least so as to be heard.

This is a light and sound effect, for the train is off-scene behind camera. During the interval, the redcap comes to him with his bag. Jerry shows him his ticket, tips him, and indicates that he is to put the bag on the train. This is in pantomime, or in words that can't be heard over the noise of the train. Then, after the redcap is gone and after the train has come to a stop, they can talk again. But with the train waiting—precious seconds going—there is a tremendous suspense which makes their words as hurried as their feelings are intense.

CHARLOTTE:

And what is the feminine for your word, Jerry? That's what I am, and with more reason. You were already married and I knew it. I walked in with my eyes wide open. You said it would make you happier.

JERRY:

And it has. I've got back my work. That's due to you.

CHARLOTTE:

I've been waiting for you to say that.

JERRY:

And I've more understanding for Tina. I'm even kinder to Isobel. It's as if having been given a look at beauty, I can no longer resent any unimportant ugliness of life. So don't blame yourself.

CHARLOTTE:

Then don't *you*.

JERRY:

It's different.

CHARLOTTE:

It's not! Shall I tell you what you've given me? On that very first day, a little bottle of perfumery made me feel important. You were my first friend. And then to be loved by you—a man like *you*—gave me such *pride*. And how I needed something to make me proud when I came home! When your camellias arrived and I knew you were thinking of me, I could have walked into a den of lions. In fact, I did, and the lions didn't hurt me.

VOICE OFF-SCENE:
All aboard!

CHARLOTTE:
So will you take back your word?

JERRY:
If you can marry this man and be content, I will.

CHARLOTTE:
I'll try, Jerry.

His train is moving now.

JERRY:
I'll look for you around every corner. Goodbye, darling.

She offers her hand, which he takes.

CHARLOTTE:
Goodbye, darling.

He swings out of scene and onto his train. The moving train lights make a flickering pattern on her face as she watches his car go by, and then she turns and walks away.

FADE OUT

FADE IN

176. INT. VALE DRAWING ROOM   DAY
      CLOSE SHOT   RADIO
from which comes the music of the Boston Symphony Orchestra playing Tchaikovsky's Fifth. Camera slowly pulls back and pans to a sofa on which, side by side, sit Charlotte and Elliot. He is deeply absorbed in the music, but her thoughts are far away. After a moment he

takes her hand. She looks at him and answers his smile
a little.

177.   CLOSE SHOT   THEIR HANDS
        as he interlaces his fingers with hers, locking her hand
        in his.

178.   THE TWO
        as he pats her locked hand with his free hand, then settles
        back, thoroughly contented and relaxed, to enjoy the
        music again. She relapses into her thoughts.
            After a moment her thoughts become disturbed. It's
        as if she is struggling against some constriction. (Let the
        music help here—some agitated, almost violent pas-
        sage of it.) No longer able to stand the constriction of
        his hand, she pulls her own hand away. This is com-
        pletely an unconscious gesture with her, but Elliot takes
        full note of it and it puzzles and disturbs him.

        ELLIOT:
            You don't like to have your hand held very much,
            do you, dear?

        CHARLOTTE (startled out of her reverie):
            Oh, yes, I do, Elliot!

        ELLIOT:
            I've noticed lately—

        CHARLOTTE:
            I've been nervous—I haven't felt myself—

        ELLIOT:
            I've noticed you always pull your hand away after
            the first few minutes.

        CHARLOTTE:
            I won't again! I'm just not used to it. You must re-
            member I'm an old maid, Elliot. You've got to teach

me to be loving and affectionate. *Make* me be! (Moves closer.) Put your arm around me.

ELLIOT:

All right, dear. (He puts his arm around her, but placidly. His hand pats her shoulder. She leans against him. The patting goes on. If it would only stop!) Do you know, dear, what we'll be doing six weeks from today?

She suddenly swings around and kneels on the floor in front of him and looks up at him with great intensity.

CHARLOTTE:

Do you know what I'd like?

ELLIOT:

What, dear? To go some place other than the Rockies for our honeymoon?

CHARLOTTE:

I'd like you to take me out to dinner some night this week, to some sort of Bohemian place, and give me a very gay time—cocktails and champagne—and then make violent love to me.[14] Then I'd know whether or not I could love you, if I wasn't quite responsible. (Falters as she sees his puzzled expression; looks away.) What I mean is, if I could only get rid of some of my inhibitions just for once, I might be able to—to have more confidence. I don't know that I can tell you. But—well, I read about a woman, in a novel—a sort of repressed woman—who was in an automobile accident with a man. It was a very cold night and they had to sit wrapped in a robe all night to keep warm. Just before they wrapped up, they both took a strong drink, and she fell in love with him because she lost her inhibitions. She was just—natural. You see—

She stops, for now there is disapproval in Elliot's expression, as if she has said something that has offended his sense of good taste. She can feel one of those familiar blushes of shame creeping up to her face.

CHARLOTTE:
It sounds sort of depraved, I'm afraid.

ELLIOT:
It certainly does! We're not that kind of people. Must we discuss such things, Charlotte?

CHARLOTTE:
No, Elliot. No. Not again.

With a stifled half-sigh she leans back against the couch, turning her face away from him. Then there is a long moment of silence between them. But neither of them is hearing the music. Now he is as disturbed as she. Then:

CHARLOTTE: ELLIOT:
Elliot—   Charlotte—

CHARLOTTE:
Which of us shall say it?

ELLIOT:
Do you think we were both going to say the same thing?

CHARLOTTE:
You say it.

ELLIOT:
Well, about our trip to the Rockies—if you're not ready yet, I could exchange the two tickets for three and take the boys.

CHARLOTTE:
Oh, would you!

ELLIOT:
Certainly. (A pause.) I've been thinking about us, Charlotte.

CHARLOTTE:
Yes.

ELLIOT:
Perhaps you're right. Perhaps we wouldn't be happy.

CHARLOTTE:
You ought to marry someone who enjoys what you enjoy—listening to the radio—and golf and riding and shooting and tennis. And someone very young, who can make a sort of older sister to your boys and join them in their sports, too.

ELLIOT (stirs):
Well—

CHARLOTTE:
Let's not linger over it, Elliot.

He helps her to her feet.

179.   ANGLE FROM HALLWAY
as they come out and camera trucks them to the front door.

ELLIOT:
I suppose you'll meet somebody sometime . . .

CHARLOTTE:
No, I don't think I shall ever marry. Some women aren't the marrying kind. But you'll meet someone. And thank you so much for thinking it was me. (Hands him his hat.) I'm glad there isn't a ring to give back.

ELLIOT:
Shall I kiss you goodbye?

CHARLOTTE:
Oh, let's not. We'll be seeing each other. We'll still be friends, won't we?

ELLIOT:
> Of course. Well, goodbye till we meet again.

CHARLOTTE:
> Goodbye, Elliot, till we meet again.

He goes out to his car, waiting in the driveway. She shuts the door and walks thoughtfully toward the stairs.

180. CRANE SHOT
taking her upstairs.

CHARLOTTE'S VOICE:
> It's like the time when my father died. His breathing just stopped. All over. Finished. Ended forever. You fool, oh, you fool! Now you will never have a home of your own or a man of your own or a child of your own.

On the first landing, before her mother's door, she stops. Well, it has to be done sometime. She goes inside.

181. INT. MRS. VALE'S ROOM
as Charlotte enters. Mrs. Vale is seated in her wheelchair by the bay window, eating her lunch from a tea table. Charlotte sits in the low rocker nearby.

MRS. VALE:
> I thought Elliot was staying for lunch. What was his hurry today?

CHARLOTTE:
> We've broken our engagement.

MRS. VALE:
> What did you say? (Then, after a pause.) Why have you done that?

CHARLOTTE:
> Because I'm not in love with him.

She is rocking gently back and forth.

MRS. VALE:

Haven't you any sense of obligation to your family
or to *me*? Here you've got a chance to join our name,
Vale, with one of the finest families in the city, Livingston, and you come in here and tell me you're
not "in love"! You talk like a romantic girl of eighteen.

CHARLOTTE (calmly):

I have no doubt of it.

MRS. VALE (infuriated):

Stop rocking! (Charlotte obeys, gets up.) You've never
done anything to make your mother proud. Nor to
make yourself proud, either. Why, I should think you
would be ashamed to be born and live all your life
as just Charlotte Vale—*Miss* Charlotte Vale.

CHARLOTTE:

I never wanted to be born. And you never wanted
me to be born either. It's been a calamity on both
sides!

182.　CLOSE SHOT　CHARLOTTE

as she goes on—bitterness bursting into flame.

CHARLOTTE:

Dr. Jaquith says tyranny is sometimes an expression
of the maternal instinct. But if that's a mother's love,
I want no part of it! (She turns and walks a step or
two away. From off-scene Mrs. Vale utters some
strangled sounds which might mean she is trying to
speak—one can't quite tell. After a moment Charlotte's figure relaxes.) Oh, Mother, don't let's quarrel. We've been getting along so well together lately.

She turns and takes a step or two toward her mother.
Camera pulls back with her, widening the angle to include Mrs. Vale. Mrs. Vale is sitting in a peculiar position in her chair, with her head to one side and her arms

limp along the chair arms, but at first Charlotte doesn't notice this.

CHARLOTTE:
> They were horrid things for me to say. I didn't mean them. I'm sorry, Mother.

And then she does notice her mother's peculiar position and she stops. After a moment she comes to Mrs. Vale and hesitantly touches her arm. Her hand recoils with a gesture as violent as if she has touched a snake. She hurries to the door.

183.   ANGLE FROM DOORWAY UP SECOND FLIGHT OF STAIRS
Charlotte stops in the doorway and calls up.

CHARLOTTE:
> Dora! Dora!

DORA'S VOICE:
> Coming!

Charlotte looks straight ahead of her, horror in her face. Dora comes out of her room and runs down the stairs. At the foot of the stairs she stops, looks at Charlotte, then past her into the room. As she goes inside:

CHARLOTTE:
> We quarreled. I did it.

DISSOLVE TO:

184.   INSERT   FUNERAL WREATH ON THE FRONT DOOR   DAY

CHARLOTTE'S VOICE:
> I killed my mother. I did it.

DISSOLVE TO:

185.   INT. DRAWING ROOM   GROUP
Camera is angling past a legal document, a will which projects into scene held by a lawyer's hand. Beyond it we see a row of relatives, Charlotte centered, and we hear the lawyer's voice singsonging.

LAWYER'S VOICE:
> And all the rest, residue and remainder of my es-
> tate, real, personal or mixed, I give, devise, and be-
> queath to my beloved daughter, Charlotte Vale.[15]

CHARLOTTE'S VOICE:
> *I did it! I did it!*

DISSOLVE TO:

186.   INT. TRAIN   CLOSE SHOT   CHARLOTTE   DAY
seated next to window. We can hear the sound of the
wheels clickety-clacking over the joints of the rails, and
they seem to be saying:

CHARLOTTE'S VOICE:
> I did it. I did it. I did it. I did it. (Charlotte leans her
> head against the windowpane, as if the cold hard-
> ness can ease her thoughts.) I've got to see Dr. Ja-
> quith. I'm going to be ill. I'll have to go to Cascade.
> Jerry, Jerry! Where are you now when I need you so
> much? (She turns away from the window and shakes
> her head, as if struggling with herself.) Get hold of
> yourself, Charlotte. Play the game!

DISSOLVE TO:

187.   OMITTED

188.   INT. RECEPTION HALL AT CASCADE
CLOSE SHOT   A SHEPHERD DOG
lying on the floor. At the sound of a door off-scene he
pricks his ears up. He gets up and, camera panning,
trots over and sniffs inquiringly at Charlotte, who has
just come in, carrying her suitcase.

CHARLOTTE:
> Hello, Butch.

The dog wags his tail joyously and Charlotte pats him.

MISS TRASK'S VOICE (from off-scene):
> Well, look who's here!

Camera pans with Charlotte as they meet.

Now, Voyager

CHARLOTTE:
Hello, Miss Trask!

MISS TRASK:
I was about to send out the police for you. The doctor wired you were coming.

CHARLOTTE:
It was a long drive. How are you?

They shake hands in most friendly fashion.

MISS TRASK:
Can't complain. Give me that. (Takes Charlotte's
suitcase.) I can't say you look sick.

CHARLOTTE:
I'm not, really. Just at loose ends.

MISS TRASK:
Glad to see you, anyway. (The camera is going with
them as they go down the hall toward a staircase.)
I've put you in the same old room—number eighteen. Thought it would make you feel at home.

CHARLOTTE:
Good old Trask.

MISS TRASK:
How's Jaquith?

CHARLOTTE:
As ever. Still handing out common sense when you
want sympathy.

MISS TRASK (calls off):
Here! Samson! (She hurries ahead with the suitcase,
and a moment later is heard to continue.) Run up
to eighteen with this. And see that everything is in
order. Open a window. Get ice water and a pitcher
of milk.

Simultaneously with this action, Charlotte has stopped

187

still and camera has stopped with her. She has stopped
because, while passing the entrance to the sun porch,
she has happened to glance in there and has seen something that has stopped her. There is a little girl in the
room who is seated at a card table which is covered with
a half-finished jigsaw puzzle. A most piteously unattractive child, the sight of whom has startled Charlotte.
This is Tina.

189.   INT. SUN PORCH   CLOSE SHOT   TINA
is just sitting, looking down at the puzzle, her chin in
her palms. Her long, straight, unattractive hair hangs
down on each side of her face like a pair of curtains. She
isn't touching a single piece of the puzzle, just sitting
there, staring down, not moving a muscle.

190.   ENTRANCE   CHARLOTTE
comes to the entrance. She still can't quite believe that
this is Jerry's child—and yet—there can't be any mistake.

191.   TWO-SHOT
For a long moment Charlotte watches Tina from the
threshold unobserved. Then slowly she walks into the
room. Halfway toward Tina, she purposely moves a chair
so that the noise will let Tina know of her presence. Tina
looks up then, quickly and suspiciously. How well
Charlotte recognizes the feelings from her own childhood that have made her look up this way. With an effort, she forces herself to be casual as she says:

CHARLOTTE:
    How is it coming?

TINA (unresponsively):
    All right.

Charlotte puts her head to one side and studies the por-
tions of the picture already fitted together.

Now, Voyager

CHARLOTTE:
What's it supposed to be?

TINA:
I don't know.

CHARLOTTE:
Here's the girl's other slipper! Mind if I join you? (Sits down.) What's the title of the picture? (Reaches for box cover.) It says "The Proposal." I think the girl is in pink. Isn't that the edge of her dress above the slipper? I'll collect all the pink pieces, unless you'd rather I wouldn't. Sometimes it's more fun to do a puzzle alone.

The child raises her eyes then, but not her chin, and looks at Charlotte. She says in a low, antagonistic tone.

TINA:
I know who you are.

CHARLOTTE (startled):
You do! Who am I?

TINA:
You're my new nurse.

CHARLOTTE:
You're wrong.

TINA:
You can't fool me. And I know why you've come here—to make sure I don't run away from this place again.

CHARLOTTE:
Did you run away from this place once? I didn't know it. What's your name, by the way?

TINA:
You know my name. That's why you stood there and stared at me.

189

CHARLOTTE:
How rude of me. But it was only because you reminded me of somebody.

TINA:
Who?

CHARLOTTE:
Well, if you must know—in lots of ways of myself.
I mean when I was your age, of course. Aren't you
about fourteen?

TINA:
I'm twelve, nearly thirteen.

MISS TRASK (comes in):
Oh, there you are. I thought I'd lost you. (Then to
Tina.) Christine, your schedule says you are to spend
your evenings with the young people.

TINA:
They don't want me.

MISS TRASK:
Of course they want you! But naturally they'd want
you more if you'd make a little effort yourself. I've
got a ping-pong game all fixed up for you. You're to
play doubles. Barbara and Betty against you and Bob.

TINA:
But he's the best player here!

MISS TRASK:
That's why you're to be his partner, so as to make it
an even match.

TINA:
Oh, but I'll be the worst one! I'll die! I'll just *die!*

MISS TRASK:
You'll do nothing of the sort. Don't dramatize,
Christine.

TINA:

Oh, please, please, please! (She beseeches with a terror-stricken expression.) Don't make me, don't make me, don't make me!

CHARLOTTE:

No, don't make her.

Miss Trask turns and looks at Charlotte in blank amazement. No one has ever interfered with her authority.

MISS TRASK:

The doctors want Christine to have exercise in the evening and I'm here—

CHARLOTTE:

I'll see that she has some exercise. I was going to ask her if she would go down to the town with me later. I want to leave my car at a garage and get it washed. We'll walk back, or *run* back, if you say so. That is, if Christine will be so kind as to go with me! Will you, Christine?

Tina studies the problem for a moment, weighing the odds between ping-pong and a stranger, alternately eyeing Miss Trask and Charlotte.

TINA:

Yes.

MISS TRASK (to Charlotte, dryly):

I thought you were too tired tonight to do anything but crawl into bed.

CHARLOTTE (just as dryly):

Cascade must have performed another miracle on me.

TINA (suddenly bursts out):

Oh, please let me go with this lady! I'll promise to drink all my cocoa tonight if you will. Upon my word of honor.

MISS TRASK:

For goodness sake, stop dramatizing, Christine! (Then abruptly.) Go get your hat and coat.

Tina shoots out of the room like a bird let out of a cage.

CHARLOTTE:

I couldn't help it.

MISS TRASK:

By the way, she's in sixteen—you're in eighteen and share the same bathroom. Don't be disturbed if you hear her crying. She has spells of it. Just ignore it. It's one of her little tyrannies—like not eating. Ignore that, too. But if you can manage to get some food into her tonight—(Breaks off.) Here she comes.

DISSOLVE TO:

192.   INT. DRUGSTORE   CHARLOTTE AND TINA   AT A TABLE
are drinking ice-cream sodas and eating Fig Newtons.

CHARLOTTE:

How long have you been at Cascade?

TINA:

Ten days—nearly eleven.

CHARLOTTE:

You don't like it much, do you?

TINA:

No.

CHARLOTTE:

Neither did I at the end of ten days. But the first two weeks are the worst.

TINA:

I shall never like it. And if they keep me here, I shall die. Then they'll be satisfied.

CHARLOTTE:

Who are "they"?

TINA:

My mother and my sister.

CHARLOTTE:

Haven't you a father?

TINA:

Yes. The reason I said I'd come here was because of my father. The doctor said it would help him.

CHARLOTTE:

Where were you headed when you tried to run away?

TINA:

For a telephone booth in the town to put in a reverse call to Daddy.

CHARLOTTE:

To ask him to come and get you?

TINA:

No. I promised him I'd stay here for two weeks. I just wanted to hear Daddy's voice. I— (She lowers her head. Several tears drop on the table.)

CHARLOTTE:

Listen, Christine, there's a telephone booth in the corner and here's my purse full of change.

TINA:

You mean I can call him now?

CHARLOTTE:

Certainly, that's what I mean. I'll wait for you here.

TINA:

Come with me, will you, please? I'm not sure I can run it.

CHARLOTTE:

All right.

They go out to:

193.   TELEPHONE BOOTH
as they enter.

CHARLOTTE:
Open my change purse, will you?

Tina opens the bag and takes out her change purse.
Charlotte deposits a coin, dials.

CHARLOTTE (into phone):
Long distance. I'd like to put in a call to—

Suddenly she stops, afraid to go on. She looks at Tina.

TINA:
Mount Vernon.

CHARLOTTE (into phone):
Mount Vernon, New York . . . Yes, that's right. Person to person to Mr.—(again stops.)

TINA:
Jeremiah Duveaux Durrance.

CHARLOTTE (into phone):
Jeremiah Duveaux Durrance. (To Tina.) Do you think
your father will be home tonight?

TINA:
I don't know.

After Charlotte listens to the operator, she deposits coins
in the phone. The quarters make a big "bong." Tina's
eyes pop.

TINA:
All of *that?*

194.   INT. CORNER OF DURRANCE LIVING ROOM   AT PHONE
CLOSE SHOT   JERRY

JERRY:
Hello . . .

195.   CHARLOTTE AND TINA
At the sound of his voice, Charlotte stiffens. She can't
say a word. She hands the receiver to Tina. Tina takes it
and Charlotte steps out of the booth.

TINA:
Hello . . . (tears of gladness choke her.) Hello,
Daddy? . . . Hello, Daddy?

Charlotte chokes up. Camera trucking, she walks swiftly
away. She sits down at their table, trembling.
DISSOLVE TO:

196.   AT BOOTH   TINA
is finishing.

TINA:
Goodbye, Daddy . . . Yes, I'll try. Goodbye. (She
hangs up and, camera trucking, runs back to the
table. Her eyes are shining, her cheeks flushed; she
looks almost pretty. The words pour out of her in a
torrent.) Oh, thank you for letting me speak to him.
Thank you, thank you! I'd like to finish my ice-cream
soda now.

CHARLOTTE:
Let's have a fresh one. (Calls off.) Two more of these,
please.

TINA:
But I'll owe you so much! Daddy said I'm to pay you
back the money. He wanted to know who was letting me call him. All I could say was "a nice light
lady" and that I'd write to him tomorrow and tell
him your name. What is your name, please?

CHARLOTTE:
Don't you think secrets rather fun? Just refer to me
as the nice light lady. It sounds so mysterious. And
look here, I don't think I'd say anything to Miss Trask
about this telephone call. It might put me in a little
wrong.

TINA:

Of course not! Nor Dr. Brine nor Dr. Jaquith. I won't tell a single living soul. I'd sooner sicken and die than put you in the wrong!

CHARLOTTE:

Tina! Really?

TINA:

You called me Tina!

CHARLOTTE:

Did I? How stupid! But isn't it a nickname for Christine?

TINA:

Yes, but nobody calls me that now except my father.

CHARLOTTE:

Well, then, I won't.

TINA:

No! Please. I want you to call me Tina!

DISSOLVE TO:

197.   INT. CHARLOTTE'S ROOM AT CASCADE   MED. SHOT
CHARLOTTE
is lying in her bed, but she is awake. She is listening with distress to the muffled sound of sobbing which comes from the adjoining room. Pretty soon she can't stand it anymore. She gets up and goes through the bathroom and into:

198.   INT. TINA'S ROOM
Charlotte comes in cautiously on tiptoe. The room is dark. The sobbing comes from the direction of the bed. Camera trucking, Charlotte goes to the bed. At first glance it appears to be empty, but there is a slight mound in the middle of the bed. Tina has crawled under the blankets and is lying curled up, face down. Charlotte sits down on the edge of the bed and places her hand on the jerk-

ing mound. Instantly it becomes motionless. All sound
ceases and the body stiffens.

CHARLOTTE:

It's only I, Tina. Don't be afraid. Tell me what's the
matter?

Charlotte is unprepared for what happens. Tina wriggles
out of her cave, half sits up and stares at Charlotte, and
when convinced of her identity, casts herself upon her,
burying her head in her lap, clinging to her, and begins
sobbing again. Charlotte puts her arms around the jerk-
ing body and slips into the bed beside Tina. She holds
her so closely to her that her own body jerks a little, too,
with each sob. She doesn't say anything. When the con-
vulsive intakes of breath are further apart and speech is
possible:

TINA:

Don't leave me.

CHARLOTTE:

I won't till you're asleep. What's the matter?

TINA (after a long pause, blurts it out):

I'm ugly and mean and nobody likes me!

CHARLOTTE:

Tina! You?

TINA:

I'm not pretty in the least, you know I'm not.

CHARLOTTE:

Whoever would want that kind of prettiness, Tina?
The kind you're born with? That's to nobody's credit.
But there's another kind you can have if you earn it.
A kind of beauty.

TINA:

What kind?

197

CHARLOTTE:

Something which has nothing to do with your face—
but which shines from a sort of light from inside
you—because you are a nice person. Think about it
and some day you'll find out I'm right.

TINA:

Will they like me then?

CHARLOTTE:

Whoever doesn't now?

TINA:

Everybody. All the kids at school . . . Miss Trask and
the nurses and the doctors. There must be something awfully wrong with me.

CHARLOTTE:

Well, do you like them? The kids at school, Miss
Trask, and the nurses and doctors?

TINA:

No! I hate them!

CHARLOTTE:

Well, here's another thought for you to grow up on.
The sure way to make people like you is for you to
like people. That's what Miss Trask means when she
tells you to cooperate. It's what Dr. Jaquith means
when he tells you to play the game.

TINA:

I'll bet you're only fooling me.

CHARLOTTE:

Well, you try and see. And in the meantime—if it
will help you—just keep remembering that *I* like
you—and I think you're pretty, and very sweet. All
right?

TINA:

All right. Why are you so good to me?

CHARLOTTE:

Lots of reasons. But one is enough. There was someone who was good to me once when I needed someone. Go to sleep now, Tina, and I'll tell you a story. Close your eyes and make your muscles all go limp and I'll tell you. That's better. Now pretend you're a child, for the story may be too young for you. Once upon a time ther was a little girl who was afraid . . .

Pan over to clock: 11:15.

DISSOLVE TO:

clock: 2 o'clock

PAN BACK TO:

199. A SIMILAR SET-UP   (SEVERAL HOURS LATER)
Charlotte is still holding Tina, who is asleep. She has been afraid to shift her position for fear it would disturb the child. She is cramped and uncomfortable. Now Tina stirs, sits up and gazes in silence at her.

CHARLOTTE:

Hello! Know me? (Tina nods emphatically.) You've had a fine sleep. If you'll let me get my arm out from under you, I'll go to my room now.

TINA:

Oh, please don't go yet—let's lie spoon-fashion. (She promptly flips over, wraps Charlotte's arms around her and locks them with her own.) This is the way Daddy and I used to lie when he'd put me to sleep when I was little. I'm too old for it now, Mother says. She says I'm too old to call him Daddy, too.

With a sigh, she is asleep again. Charlotte holds her close. After a long moment:

CHARLOTTE'S VOICE:
This is Jerry's child in my arms. This is Jerry's child clinging to me.

FADE OUT

FADE IN

200. EXT. CASCADE   TRUCKING SHOT   DR. JAQUITH   (DAY)
comes out of one of the buildings and walks along the driveway toward a tennis court. Apparently he is in a rage. He keeps mumbling to himself.

DR. JAQUITH:
Impertinent . . . Upsetting rules . . . Thinks she can run the works . . .

201. MED. LONG SHOT
approaching the tennis court.

202. TENNIS COURT   CHARLOTTE AND TINA
playing, neither awfully well. Tina flubs a shot.

TINA:
Oh, I'm terrible!

CHARLOTTE:
Of course you are. So am I. What difference? We'll learn.

Dr. Jaquith walks right up to Charlotte.

DR. JAQUITH:
I want to talk to you!

CHARLOTTE:
Me? (Dr. Jaquith jerks his head, indicating that Charlotte is to follow him.) I thought you might. (He strides off the court and she does follow.)

203. TRUCKING SHOT   DR. JAQUITH AND CHARLOTTE
walk away from the tennis court. He strides two steps ahead of her and his expression is very grim and forbid-

ding. Charlotte is doing some thinking. How will she handle this? But it isn't worried thinking. Possibly she even makes a motion of wanting to hit Dr. Jaquith over the head with her tennis racquet. Anyway, her spirit is that determined.

204.   TINA
looks off at them, frightened.

205.   DR. JAQUITH AND CHARLOTTE
reach a little shelter, a sort of covered seat, and go around in front of it. Suddenly he turns on her. He keeps his voice low on account of Tina, but his tone is pretty fierce just the same.

DR. JAQUITH:
    I hear *you*'re running Cascade now.

CHARLOTTE:
    Now, Dr. Jaquith—

DR. JAQUITH:
    You give orders to my doctors. You give orders to Miss Trask—

CHARLOTTE:
    I didn't give orders. I requested.

DR. JAQUITH:
    I thought you came up here to have a nervous breakdown.

CHARLOTTE:
    I've decided not to have it, if it's all the same to you.

We can see now that most of Dr. Jaquith's anger is bluff. His eyes are twinkling.

DR. JAQUITH:
    Well, since you're no longer my patient—since you've become a member of my staff, Doctor—

Now, Voyager

CHARLOTTE:
Oh, I know I've been impertinent—

DR. JAQUITH:
Go ahead, Maybe I like it.

CHARLOTTE:
The child is terribly unhappy here and I don't think she's being treated wisely. Usually I'm proud of you, but this time I'm ashamed.

DR. JAQUITH:
Then isn't it wonderful you know so much better.

CHARLOTTE:
I have a proposition to make to you. I'm not doing anything with my time. Mightn't *I* do instead of a nurse? I promise not to break any more rules without asking first. If you'll only—

DR. JAQUITH:
I've already canceled the nurse. Just go ahead—tell me what you'd do.

CHARLOTTE:
I'd just be with her. I'd pay her attention and make her feel wanted and important. As soon as you'd let me, I'd take her away on a trip—to the woods—she loves the woods.

DR. JAQUITH:
Sounds like a wonderful break for her.

CHARLOTTE:
Of course, I couldn't without her parents' consent. And I wouldn't. What would her mother say, do you suppose?

DR. JAQUITH:
She'd accept any plan which relieves her of the child, who has always been a thorn in her flesh—though

202

the lady would strongly protest if she heard me say
so.

CHARLOTTE:

And the father? Should I know his attitude toward
Christine?

DR. JAQUITH:

Sympathetic and protective—probably too protective for Christine's good. Result, resentment felt by
the mother. Result, the father has always defended
the child against the mother and the world generally. Result, the child has developed an abnormal
devotion for the father. Result, the mother has developed jealousy of the child. Result, the child's absence from the home becomes desirable for all concerned. Result, I bring her here. I'd been highly
recommended to the father by a friend of his. But,
of course, he placed the child in my care—not in
yours . . .

CHARLOTTE (after a slight pause):
I suppose I had better ask you a question. How much
do you know about South America?

DR. JAQUITH:
Well, geographically—

CHARLOTTE:

You know what I mean. My automobile accident and
the man who was with me. In New York you said
he helped me out of one difficulty and into another.

DR. JAQUITH:

Well, a patient of mine who has a phobia about high
places told me about an accident happening to a man
and woman who were in Brazil when she was there.
She knew the woman's name, though not the man's.
In fact, she told me the woman's name before I could
stop her.

CHARLOTTE:

And who told you the man's name?

DR. JAQUITH:

Nobody. I don't know his name.

CHARLOTTE:

You didn't know that Christine's father and I had met before?

It stops him cold. It takes him by surprise, and far from pleasantly so. After a long pause:

DR. JAQUITH:

No, I didn't know. (Then.) If I had known, I certainly wouldn't have advised you to come to Cascade at present. I had no idea you had ever even met Durrance! (His tone is extremely hostile.)

CHARLOTTE:

You mean this alters the whole situation? But you just admitted—

DR. JAQUITH:

I don't know anything about your relationship with Durrance. I don't know how emotionally involved you are with him. I can't work in the dark when there's a child in the picture.

CHARLOTTE:

I'll tell you everything. It's over. That's everything in two words. Dr. Jaquith, Tina needs me as much as she did a minute ago. I've never been needed before!

He thinks it over for what seems to her a long time.

DR. JAQUITH:

Well, I'm crazy—If you promise to behave yourself—

CHARLOTTE:

I'll tell her! (Starts away.)

DR. JAQUITH (calls after her):
But you're only on probation! Remember what it says in the Bible: "The Lord giveth and the Lord taketh away"!

CHARLOTTE (calls back):
How does it feel to be the Lord?

DR. JAQUITH:
No so very wonderful since the free will bill was passed. Too little power.

DISSOLVE TO:

206. A PUBLIC TELEPHONE BOOTH   CHARLOTTE AND TINA
The child is talking to her father. Charlotte is standing close, to hear his voice.

TINA:
. . . and I'm not going to have a nurse! I'm just going to have her. She'll be my—(To Charlotte.) What *are* you?

CHARLOTTE (quietly, with a smile):
Your friend.

TINA (into phone again):
And I can tell you her name now. She said I could. Her name is Miss Vale—not the kind you wear on your face—but V-A-L-E—and she's from Boston and she's ever so nice . . . What's that, Daddy? (To Charlotte.) He said to tell you thank you.

CHARLOTTE:
I heard him.

TINA:
Would you like to speak to him?

She offers the receiver to Charlotte. It takes her a long moment to resist the temptation.

CHARLOTTE:
No, thank you.

TINA (into phone):
> She won't talk to you. I think she's quite shy. Oh, Daddy, do you know something? Pretty soon—when the doctor says it's all right—she's going to take me away. Just she and I—

DISSOLVE TO:

206A.   MONTAGE
The purpose of this montage is to show the healthy mental and physical improvement in Tina, due to her close association with Charlotte.

(1) CHARLOTTE'S CAR   COUNTRY ROAD   DAY
Charlotte and Tina are in the car. They are dressed for roughing it, and the car is loaded with miscellaneous camping equipment.

(2) MED. SHOT   CHARLOTTE AND TINA   (PROCESS)

CHARLOTTE (very gay as she tries to draw Tina out of herself):
> Isn't this fun, Tina! We're as free as *birds!*

TINA:
> I wish I was a bird. (Wistfully.) Birds are pretty.

CHARLOTTE (forcing gaiety above the compassion the child's remark arouses):
> Never mind how we look—we can *fly.*

(3) CLOSE-UP   TINA
as she smiles timidly. Camera pans down to spinning car wheel. Over this we superimpose

CLOSE SHOT   MILEAGE INDICATOR ON CAR'S DASHBOARD
as the miles roll by.

DISSOLVE TO:

(4) CLOSE-UP OF FLAT TIRE
Camera pulls back to a scene of Charlotte and Tina changing a tire and actually having fun doing it.

DISSOLVE TO:

(4A) THE SPINNING TIRE
with the mileage indicator again telling off the miles.

(5) BEAUTIFUL HILLSIDE LANDSCAPE   DAY

Charlotte and Tina are running hand in hand up the slope toward camera. They are laughing as they run, and the breeze rustling the grass about them whips their hair into madcap halos. As they near the crest Charlotte, exhausted, falls laughing in the grass, pulling Tina down with her.

(6) CLOSE SHOT   CHARLOTTE AND TINA

as Charlotte pants for breath.

TINA (eagerly):
Come on, Miss Vale, you said we'd run to the *top*. This isn't the top!

CHARLOTTE (ruefully):
I guess I should have said we'd *walk* to the top.

DISSOLVE TO:

(7) A MOUNTAIN STREAM

Charlotte and Tina are fishing on either side of a log. Charlotte's line jerks.

CHARLOTTE (excitedly):
I have a bite!

As she pulls upon her line, Tina's pole jerks.

TINA (also excited):
Me too!

They both pull frantically.

(8) INSERT OF LINES UNDER LOG

The two hooks are tangled together, and it is evident that Tina and Charlotte are only pulling against each other.

DISSOLVE TO:

(9) OMITTED

(10) A BEAUTIFUL NIGHT SKY WITH STARS AGAINST
TREETOPS
Camera pans slowly down to Charlotte and Tina peacefully asleep in a sleeping bag. Tina's head is on Charlotte's arm. Camera continues past them to the dying
embers of a campfire.

DISSOLVE TO:

207–208. A CAMP IN THE WOODS   LATE EVENING
A very simple affair, just Charlotte's car and a tent pitched
beside it. A campfire before the tent at which Tina is
roasting potatoes. Tina is dressed for roughing it, in
denim, her hair all pushed up under a tam.

TINA (calls):
    Miss Vale!

CHARLOTTE'S VOICE (from inside tent):
    What's cooking?

TINA:
    Potatoes! And they're *cooked*.

CHARLOTTE'S VOICE:
    They smell good.

She comes out of the tent. She carries a half-completed
letter which she has been writing.

TINA:
    What have you been doing?

CHARLOTTE:
    Writing a letter.

TINA:
    A secret?

CHARLOTTE:
    What's secret between us? It's to Dr. Jaquith, asking
    if I can keep you a little while longer. When I go
    back to Boston this fall, I want to take you with me

208

to the big house on Marlborough Street. Would you like that?

TINA:
It would be very elegant. Here.

She hands Charlotte a potato. Charlotte takes it, drops it, for it is very hot.

CHARLOTTE:
Ooh! Let that cool off!

TINA:
Oh, I'm sorry. (She takes Charlotte's hand and kisses her fingers.)

CHARLOTTE:
It would be sort of like playing house.

TINA:
Are you old enough to be my mother?

CHARLOTTE:
Heavens, yes!

TINA:
I wish you were my mother. Suddenly Tina is in Charlotte's arms.

CHARLOTTE (rather sternly):
No, you don't, Tina. You mustn't think that.

TINA:
You don't act like a mother. You don't tell me what to do or what not to do all the time. I wish I didn't have to call you "Miss Vale." It sounds funny—as if we didn't know each other very well.

CHARLOTTE:
How would you like to call me some nickname, or special name of our own, as if we were sort of chums?

TINA:
I'd love it! What special name?

CHARLOTTE:
My first name, Charlotte, has all sorts of abbrevia-
tions. You might call me Carlotta or Charlie or—a
name I was called once in fun—Camille. Or, if you'd
rather, Auntie, or Tante. Or even Aunt Charlotte.
Think it over.

TINA:
I guess I'll call you Camille. It's kind of a funny name,
though.

FADE OUT

FADE IN

208A. EXT. THE VALE HOME LONG SHOT (LATE AFTERNOON)

DISSOLVE TO:

208B. INT. TINA'S STUDIO CLOSE SHOT A COCKER SPANIEL
is disconsolately posed on a brocade chair by a window.
Camera pulls back to include Tina, who is working at an
easel on a half-completed portrait in crayons of the dog.
The portrait is not really professional, but it is good
enough to indicate promising signs of talent in the young
artist. Tina is dressed from shoulders to knees in a dark
blue smock. Her hair is done up in curlers. There are
smudges of crayon on her face. The braces are gone from
her teeth, but she still wears her glasses. There is a certain charm in her appearance, but it does not spring from
beauty.

TINA (is saying):
Cheer up, Bingo, and just be patient, and maybe
someday we'll both be famous.

CHARLOTTE'S VOICE (from hallway outside):
Tina?

TINA:
Cam-eel! I'm right in here.

CHARLOTTE (comes in):
Well, how's it coming with my budding Rosa Bon-
heur?

TINA:

All right, I guess. But Bingo is getting pretty sick of it.

CHARLOTTE (solemnly, half joking):

I guess Bingo doesn't understand the seriousness of artistic creation. (Charlotte sits in a chair. Her expression is rather serious.) Come here, darling. I have something to tell you. (Rubs smudge off her nose, then goes on seriously.) Your father telephoned today.

TINA:

How is Daddy?

CHARLOTTE:

Fine. He asked if he might fly up with Dr. Jaquith and have dinner with us tonight.

Across Tina's face crosses a series of expressions in this order: pleasure, perplexity, suspicion, and finally, terror.

CHARLOTTE:

What's the matter, Tina?

TINA:

Why is my father coming?

CHARLOTTE:

Just to have dinner and see what sort of place you're staying in.

TINA:

Then why didn't he say so in his last letter? I know why he's coming! I know! He's going to take me home! (She buries her face in Charlotte's shoulder and bursts into violent crying.) Oh, don't make me go!

Charlotte holds Tina in her arms reassuringly and comfortingly.

CHARLOTTE:
>No, Tina . . . Darling, don't cry. We'll talk about it. Your Daddy loves you as I love you . . . [16]
>>DISSOLVE TO:

FADE IN

209.   EXT. VALE HOME   LONG SHOT   EVENING JUST GETTING DARK

A taxicab is pulling up the driveway. It stops before the house.

210.   AT TAXICAB   DR. JAQUITH AND JERRY

get out. Both are in dinner coats. Dr. Jaquith carries a roll of blueprints under his arm. As Jerry pays off the driver:

DR. JAQUITH:
>Ever been in this house before?

JERRY:
>You know I haven't.

They walk up toward the front door.

DR. JAQUITH:
>It's a gloomy old pile. How anyone can bear to live in it is more than I know. (Rings bell.)

JERRY:
>Tina writes me she lives here like a princess in a palace.

DR. JAQUITH:
>Yes? Well, I suppose it feeds her starved sense of self-importance.

The door is opened by William. A burst of music comes out.

211.   INT. HALLWAY

Judging from it, and you can safely judge from it, the Marlborough Street house has undergone a complete

transformation. The heavy wood has been lightened.
There is air, brightness, and happiness. It is a friendly
house. And the house gives forth new sounds—music
and giggling of youngsters, and laughter from the
drawing room. Dr. Jaquith stares as he and Jerry come
in and surrender their hats to William.

JERRY:
I thought you said gloom.

CHARLOTTE'S VOICE (off-scene):
Hello, there! Welcome! (She enters swiftly and, because he is nearest, goes first to Dr. Jaquith.) How
are you, Doctor?

DR. JAQUITH:
I'm amazed. What's been going on here?

CHARLOTTE:
A little redoing—whatever is the opposite of aging.
(Then to Jerry.) I'm awfully glad you came up, Mr.
Durrance.

JERRY:
I'm awfully glad you let me.

Camera follows them as she takes them in.

CHARLOTTE:
Tina's well. I told her you were coming.

JERRY:
Was she pleased?

CHARLOTTE (thoughtfully):
Yes . . . but terrified, too. She's afraid you're coming
to take her home. That isn't meant against you—
you know that—but treat her carefully, will you?

As they reach the entrance to the drawing room June
bursts out.

JUNE:

> Charlotte—(Stops as she sees men.) Oh, excuse me. Why, hello, Dr. Jaquith.

CHARLOTTE:

> You remember June?

DR. JAQUITH:

> Who could forget?

CHARLOTTE:

> And this is Mr. Durrance.

JUNE:

> Tina's father? Peachy! (Then to Charlotte.) Nicholas phoned from across the river. He wants to know if he can come to dinner. He just found out his mother is having one of those *formal* things. (Makes a face.) He can be here in ten minutes. Is it all right?

CHARLOTTE:

> Of course it's all right.

JUNE:

> If there's enough grub, he'll bring Chad and Hank along.

CHARLOTTE:

> Well, you'd better tell Cook to start cutting the squabs in two. (To Jerry and Jaquith.) This goes on all the time.

DR. JAQUITH:

> What *does* go on here?

He is looking into the drawing room. Through the entrance we can see part of the room. It is as transformed as the hallway. Three youngsters of approximately June's age, two girls and a boy, are around the fireplace, roasting things with long forks. There are also a couple of dogs and a cat in the room.

JUNE:
We're roasting weenies.

DR. JAQUITH:
Roasting weenies?

CHARLOTTE (with a laugh):
And in Mother's fireplace, too!

June takes Dr. Jaquith's arm and leads him in.

JUNE (to Jaquith):
Weenies make swell canapes. Come on, pet, you can
roast, too. I'll make you known to my gang.

TINA'S VOICE (from upstairs, squealing):
Cam-eel! Cam-eel!

Charlotte and Jerry look up.

212. STAIRWAY   A LITTLE DOG
(probably a cocker) runs down frantically.

213. ANGLE FROM STAIRWAY   CHARLOTTE AND JERRY

CHARLOTTE:
Tina, don't run, dear. You'll rip your dress.

She snatches the dog and gathers it up in her arms. Jerry
is staring up the stairway.

214. STAIRWAY   TINA
walks down. You wouldn't know her. She seems all at
once a young lady. She wears a long dress, pumps with
grown-up heels, and silk stockings. Her hair is cut and
fixed in a soft and pretty way about her face. She walks
down slowly, like the princess she imagines herself to
be.

215. AT FOOT OF STAIRS
Jerry stares, and his eyes are misty. Charlotte's eyes are
on Jerry's face.

216.   PAN SHOT   TINA
bringing her to them. Jerry takes her in his arms. Tina
throws her arms around him.

TINA:
    Hello, Daddy . . .

It is an inadequate little speech, but her voice is pleased
and excited and happy, and her eyes are shining. Jerry
releases her and hold her off at arm's length.

JERRY:
    Can this be Tina?

TINA:
    Do I look nice? It's a new dress. I've got grown-up
    heels.

JERRY:
    You look lovely.

TINA:
    Do you really like me?

She turns around slowly for him to see. Jerry takes her
in his arms again. He looks across her head at Charlotte.

JERRY (his eyes misty):
    I love you.

CHARLOTTE (breaks the spell):
    Take him upstairs, Tina, and show him everything.
    Show him your room and the studio—

TINA:
    Would you like to see my room, Daddy? (Takes the
    dog from Charlotte.)

JERRY:
    Very much—if Miss Vale will excuse us.

CHARLOTTE:
    Yes, but don't stay too long, Tina.

Tina takes her father's arm and they start upstairs.

TINA:
How long are you going to call her "Miss Vale"?

JERRY:
What should I call her?

TINA:
I don't know. (Then she looks back at Charlotte.)
Would it sound too funny if Daddy should call you
my name for you, Camille?

CHARLOTTE (quietly):
I think it would sound very nice indeed.

DISSOLVE TO:

217.   DRAWING ROOM
In background are the young people, the crowd now
increased by three boys and another girl. Some are
roasting weenies, others dancing to phonograph music.
In foreground, at a desk, Dr. Jaquith and Charlotte are
going over his blueprints, that is, she is: he is looking at
her with a rather peculiar expression.

CHARLOTTE:
They look fine. What are you going to call the children's building?

DR. JAQUITH:
I ought to name it after you, since it's your interest
and time and money that has made it possible. I'm
putting you on the board of directors. You knew I
would.

CHARLOTTE (catches his look):
What are you looking at, Dr. Owl?

DR. JAQUITH:
I'm just wondering—are you the same woman who,
a few months ago, hadn't a single interest in the
world?

CHARLOTTE (with a smile):
No.

Tina has entered and now comes to them.

TINA:
Well, I showed him everything and now he's gone
into the library, he says to think things out.

CHARLOTTE:
Oh? He should join the party. (Rises.) Take care of
Dr. Jaquith. (Goes out.)

TINA:
That's a funny thing to tell me. How do you take
care of a doctor? A doctor is supposed to take care
of you.

218.   HALLWAY   CHARLOTTE
crosses and goes into:

219.   INT. LIBRARY
The room is dark, lit only by the light from the hallway
door and the glow from the cannel-coal fire in the fireplace. Jerry has been standing, staring down at the coals,
but he turns as Charlotte comes in.

CHARLOTTE:
We're all wondering what you're thinking out.

He doesn't immediately answer. She walks to him. Their
eyes meet and there is a slight pause.

JERRY:
I've decided to take Tina home.

CHARLOTTE:
Take her home! (She walks back to the door and closes
it, then comes back.) But you can't. Dr. Jaquith says
it would be the worst thing in the world for Tina to
go home now.

JERRY:

> I don't care what he says. No self-respecting man could allow such self-sacrifice as yours to go on indefinitely.

CHARLOTTE:

> That's the most conventional, pretentious, pious speech I ever heard you make in your life, Jerry! Why, I simply don't know you!

JERRY:

> I can't go on forever taking, taking, taking from you, and giving nothing, darling.

CHARLOTTE:

> Oh, I know. Forgive me, Jerry. (She sits down. A pause.) Let me explain. You *will* be giving. Don't you know that "to take" is a way "to give" sometimes—the most beautiful way in the world if two people love each other? Besides, Jerry, you'll be giving me Tina. Every single day *I'll* be taking, taking, taking, and you'll be giving.

JERRY:

> It's kind of you to put it that way.

CHARLOTTE:

> Jerry, is it Isobel? Has she begun to resent me?

JERRY:

> Isobel blesses you every day of her life. She believes you are an answer to prayer, sent by God himself in response to her fervent pleadings when Tina first went to Cascade.

CHARLOTTE:

> Is it because of something Tina has said, then? Don't you think she's happy here?

JERRY:

> Happy! She confessed to me upstairs that she thought she loved you almost as much as she did me.

CHARLOTTE:

Then what *is* your reason? Jerry, is it something about us?

JERRY (violently):

Of course it's about us! What would it be?

Then abruptly he gets up and walks to the front windows, camera panning. From the drawing room now the music has changed. It is not longer jazz, but something semiclassical. Charlotte follows him to the windows.

CHARLOTTE (quietly):

I wish you'd tell me.

JERRY:

Why didn't you marry Livingston? I'll tell you why. I came along and ruined him for you.

CHARLOTTE:

Yes—

JERRY:

And now my child comes along and claims all your attention, and takes your whole life—when you should be trying to find some man who will make you happy.

CHARLOTTE:

Some man to make me happy! So that's it. Here I have been living under the delusion that you and I were so in sympathy—so *one* that you knew without being told what would make me happy. Apparently you haven't the slightest conception of the torture it is to love a man, as I've loved you, and to be shut out—barred out—to be forever just an outsider, and an *extra!* (He tries to speak, but she goes right on.) Why, when Tina wanted to come home with me and stay, it was like a miracle happening— like my having your child—a part of *you*. And I allowed myself to indulge in the fancy that both of us loving her, and doing what was best for her together, would make her seem actually like our child after a while. But no such fancy has occurred to you, I see! Again I've been just a big, sentimental fool! It's a tendency I have!

She turns away from him but he takes her by the shoulders and turns her back. As she starts to speak again:

JERRY:
Wait a minute.

Pinioning her arms to her sides, he holds her straight in front of him an arm's length away. His strength is, as ever, a source of surprise to Charlotte.

CHARLOTTE (quietly):
Please let me go.

But he doesn't let her go.

JERRY:
Now I know. It won't die—what's between us. Do what we will—ignore it, neglect it, starve it—it's stronger than both of us together. Oh, Charlotte—

He slips his hands slowly down her arms to her wrists. She feels again the old sense of joy. But she mustn't give in to it. If she lets him kiss her now, all her resolutions will be swept away.

CHARLOTTE:
Let me go. (Her voice is desperate now. There is a little struggle and she breaks free. He turns away toward the window. After a moment she makes a half-gesture toward him, but draws it back. There are tears in her eyes now.) Jerry . . . Dr. Jaquith knows about us. When he let me take Tina, he said, "You're on probation." You know what he means. I'm on probation because of you and me. He allowed this visit of yours, but it's a test. If I can't stand such

tests, I'll lose Tina in time. And we'll lose each other. Jerry, please help me.

For a minute he doesn't answer. Then he takes out his cigarette case and turns back to her.

JERRY:
Shall we just have a cigarette on it?

CHARLOTTE:
Thank you.

With the cigarettes they repeat the intimate little ceremony we have seen them go through on the balcony of the hotel at Petropolis.

JERRY:
May I sometimes come here?

CHARLOTTE:
Whenever you like. It's your home, too. People who love you live here.

JERRY:
And may I look at you and Tina—and share with you the peace that comes from contentment?

CHARLOTTE:
Yes, Jerry.

JERRY:
And sometimes smoke a cigarette with you and sit in understanding silence?

CHARLOTTE:
Always—not for this time only. We can always light our cigarettes from the same flame—that is, if you'll help me to keep what we have, if we both try hard to protect the little strip of territory that's been given us. I can talk to you once in a while about your child—

JERRY (with a whimsical smile):
   Our child.

She draws her breath in sharply as if he has touched a nerve.

CHARLOTTE:
   Thank you.

JERRY:
   And will you be happy, Charlotte? Will it be enough?

CHARLOTTE:
   Oh, Jerry, don't let's ask for the moon! We have the stars!

The camera pans up and away from them to the window. The stars are very bright in the sky.
FADE OUT

T H E   E N D

Notes to the Screenplay

1 By showing Mrs. Vale angrily reprimanding the servant William, the film's characterization of her suggests a more irritable and bossy matriarch than does the Revised Final screenplay. The Revised Final screenplay heightens the melodramatic quality by polarizing her against the "good mothering" that Charlotte and Dr. Jaquith exhibit. Presenting Mrs. Vale as rude or at least difficult with the servants establishes her character even before the family is introduced; her relationships with both are similar.

2 The film has Mrs. Vale utter two commands to Charlotte in this sequence that parallel the commands given Leslie Trotter by the ship's captain, suggesting that Mrs. Vale has a similar hold on her daughter whom she treats as a servant and recalcitrant employee. These references prepare for Charlotte's careful distinction in the scene in which she confronts her mother with her browbeating behavior. Mrs. Vale adjusts Charlotte's role from servant, to unpaid employee, to guest, to legal ward depending upon which is the least powerful position in a particular situation.

3 Bette Davis's emotional power as an actress suggests the alterations made here between Revised Final screenplay and film: from a series of mild questions in the screenplay to the ranting power of repeating the word "torturing" as Davis builds the scene to the outburst that suggests a "nervous breakdown." Like Davis's clothing, this scene and speech in particular, featuring the famous Davis gesture of the "bugging eyes," which here suggest hysteria, required a more exaggerated mode than "Do you enjoy being disagreeable?"

4 This scene of transforming the dowdy spinster Charlotte into the svelte chic young woman is not in the film, although a similar one was present in the novel. The film tends to eliminate short scenes in diverse spaces and times that were in the script. It may be that showing the machinery of the change—plucking the eyebrows, setting the hair—would have been less effective than again presenting Charlotte from the feet up in "before-and-after" fashion. It was enough to present Bette Davis as so unglamorous a character on the screen, however briefly; to linger over the explanation of the change may have subdued its magic.

5 Instead of the insert of a radiogram, the film has a flashback of Jaquith seeing Charlotte off on the boat. It reinforces his role as reas-
suring father with his Polonius-like advice (Charlotte is dressed in
subdued but stylish black and listening dutifully) and underlines
his role in achieving Charlotte's transformation. As in this example,
the film tends to diminsh the significance of women role models
and enlarge that of male father figures.

6 After this sentence in the film Charlotte adds, "In fact, they're perfectly ridiculous" and, after the next, "Only it's funnier than you
realize." Davis could have added the lines, since they intensify the
character's judgment and disgust with herself and prepare for the
tears on the boat deck—a more intensified emotional reaction than
that called for in the Revised Final but one suggested by Charlotte's
line that she has not yet recovered from her nervous breakdown.
Charlotte cries four times in the film, a record matched only by Tina
who seems to be on the verge of hysteria much of the time. Of
course, they are the ones sent to Cascade. Male composure is main-
tained throughout.

7 This line is not in the fillm, for two possible reasons. First, it would
be difficult to imagine Bette Davis's uttering this line, particularly in
this phase of her star persona's development. Second, Goulding had
suggested that the heroine must be a powerful figure repressed,
rather than a weak one easily manipulated.

8 Scenes 66–68 and 73–77 are not in the film. The Revised Final stream-
lined earlier versions considerably, but the film comparison evi-
dences even more simplification: less crosscutting between Jerry and
Charlotte in their respective cabins. The film abbreviates this seg-
ment into a single shot of Charlotte sleeping somewhat fitfully and
Jerry writing to his daughter about Charlotte. Charlotte does not
relapse into Aunt Charlotte at the mirror or dance with Leslie. This
certainly makes the sequence less choppy. Instead, the scene of
Charlotte's meeting Jerry includes a superimposition-style flashback
of Mrs. Vale lecturing Charlotte at twenty on the evils of tourists'
mentality. The moment spurs her into adventuring and reinforces
the film's presentation of Charlotte's steady steps toward self-
realization, probably satisfying the audience expectations that Davis's star personality was cultivating. The elimination of the dream-
sequence flashback not only removes an obstacle to the film's on-
ward-moving quick pacing, but privileges the single extended flashback to Charlotte on shipboard at twenty as the key explanation of

the trauma which the film solves, the enigma which it unwinds in the fashion Marc Vernet has suggested.

9 The whole sequence of Jerry and Charlotte in the cabin is greatly shortened in the film. The conversation about Tina, which had been in versions since the book, is gone, making Tina's existence almost entirely limited to the final reel except for the briefest of references. In the film Charlotte's head is near Jerry's but not on his chest, and it is he who awakens and kisses her very lightly in her sleep. Hays Office restrictions are the most obvious explanation for these omissions, including awkward "morning-after" conversation. The scene's ellipses of the declining fire and cut to a restaurant terrace are standard Hollywood Hays Office fare.

10 The airport farewell occurs in chronological order rather than as a flashback. Doing so allows for the dramatic value of their farewell (actually one of several emotional farewells) to be built from the previous scenes rather than inserted when it would interrupt the momentum that builds toward Charlotte's confronting her mother.

11 After this speech Mrs. Vale tells Charlotte about her will, which "will make you wealthy and powerful." This change is consistent with earlier ones that portray Mrs. Vale as a more explicitly manipulative adversary figure for Charlotte.

12 The film omits Charlotte's attempts at finding out about Jerry or communicating with him. Only the letter to Jaquith remains, thus delaying only slightly the showdown between Charlotte and Elliot. Like other omissions of inserts or flashbacks, this one prevents the film's pace from lagging or becoming choppy.

13 The film omits this line, which seems to me an important one for characterizing their relationship. It acknowledges that Mrs. Vale is a powerful personality who probably has rarely met her match, and that to be a tyrant, one must have a victim. A series of changes in the Revised Final suggests that Mrs. Vale's character has been altered to heighten her "villainy" or at least to portray her as a less sympathetically worthy opponent. Gladys Cooper's portrayal survives these emendations, however.

14 Three changes from script to film alter Charlotte and Elliot's relationship. Charlotte doesn't complain that Elliot hasn't made love to her (scene 159), Elliot doesn't kiss her (160), and Charlotte doesn't argue for alcohol-induced release of inhibitions (178). While the first and last can easily be attributed to Hays Office-anticipated self-censorship, the absence of the kiss underscores the lack "of pas-

226

sion" in their relationship or the image of faithlessness in a movie that presents adultery, however sanitized or obtuse.

15 The film states the amount each son receives ($3,000) while Charlotte inherits the balance of Mrs. Vale's estate. Though minor it's an interesting detail to have taken the trouble to establish. It makes clear how great Charlotte's inheritance is likely to be: guilt on the one hand but simultaneously the wherewithal to build a new wing at Cascade. This financial altruism allows her to emerge as more of a partner to Jaquith—literally, a member of the board of directors, as well as a "mother" to Tina.

16 Omitting this scene from the film hardly seems crucial, since it adds no information that the camping trip did not provide and contains too much insignificant dialogue. The audience is mercifully spared Tina's last demonstration of hysteria.

Production Credits

Produced by	Hal B. Wallis
Directed by	Irving Rapper
Screenplay by	Casey Robinson
Based on the novel by	Olive Higgins Prouty
Music by	Max Steiner
Director of Photography	Sol Polito
Film Editor	Warren Low
Art Director	Robert Haas
Montages by	Don Siegel
Sound by	Robert B. Lee
Set Decorations by	Fred M. MacLean
Dialogue Director	Edward Blatt
Special Effects by	Willard VanEnger A.S.C.
Gowns by	Orry-Kelly
Makeup Artist	Perc Westmore
Orchestral Arrangements by	Hugo Friedhofer
Musical Director	Leo F. Forbstein

Running time: 117 minutes
Released: October 31, 1942

Cast

Charlotte Vale	Bette Davis
Jerry Durrance	Paul Henreid
Dr. Jaquith	Claude Rains
Mrs. Vale	Gladys Cooper
June Vale	Bonita Granville
Elliot Livingston	John Loder
Lisa Vale	Ilka Chase
"Deb" McIntyre	Lee Patrick
Mr. Thompson	Franklin Pangborn
Miss Trask	Katherine Alexander
Frank McIntyre	James Rennie
Dora Pickford	Mary Wickes
Tina Durrance	Janis Wilson
Manoel	Frank Puglia
Dr. Dan Regan	Michael Ames
Leslie Trotter	Charles Drake
William	David Clyde

Inventory

The following materials from the Warner library of the Wisconsin Center for Film and Theater Research were used by Allen in preparing *Now, Voyager* for the Wisconsin/Warner Bros. Screenplay Series:

Novel, by Olive Higgins Prouty, 1941, 340 pages.

Treatment, by Edmund Goulding, no date, 15 pages.

Temporary, by Casey Robinson, February 19 to March 4, 1942, incomplete, 114 pages.

Final, by Robinson, March 25 to March 26 with revisions to April 3, 1942, approximately 170 pages.

Revised Final, by Robinson, April 8 with revisions to June 9, 1942, approximately 170 pages.

DESIGNED BY GARY GORE
COMPOSED BY GRAPHIC COMPOSITION, INC.
ATHENS, GEORGIA
MANUFACTURED BY INTER-COLLEGIATE PRESS, INC.
SHAWNEE MISSION, KANSAS
TEXT AND DISPLAY LINES ARE SET IN PALATINO

Library of Congress Cataloging in Publication Data
Robinson, Casey.
Now, voyager.

(Wisconsin/Warner Bros. screenplay series)
Screenplay by Casey Robinson from a novel by
Olive Higgins Prouty.
I. Allen, Jeanne Thomas. II. Prouty, Olive Higgins,
1882–   . Now, voyager. III. Title. IV. Series.
PN1997.N68   1984   791.43'72   84-40144
ISBN 0-299-09790-0
ISBN 0-299-09794-3 (pbk.)